To Mc

love Les son
Trevor
xx oo

SILENT HEROES

1" SNOW EVE of XMAS 04

SILENT HEROES

Ordinary People in Times of War

Compiled by
JOHN D. MILLER

SAINT ANDREW PRESS
Edinburgh

First published in 2004 by
SAINT ANDREW PRESS
121 George Street, Edinburgh EH2 4YN

Reprinted 2004

Copyright © John D. Miller, 2004

ISBN 0 7152 0815 2

British Library Cataloguing in Publication Date
A catalogue record for this book
is available from the British Library

Typeset by Waverley Typesetters, Galashiels
Printed and bound by Bell & Bain Ltd, Glasgow

Contents

Introduction

The purpose of this book is well illustrated in the life of a man called Patrick Hamilton, who lived in Glasgow's Castlemilk housing scheme. He died in July 2003 at the age of seventy-six. For forty-four years Pat worked with the railway, and was finally promoted to the post of supervisor of the carriage cleaners in Glasgow's Cowlairs Depot. Until he retired he worked the pattern of three shifts, and his relaxation was going to the Railway Club with his wife Nan. In the last years of his life Pat was admired by neighbours for his devoted care of Nan. She suffered from severe arthritis and could not leave the house. Pat did everything. He did the shopping, the cooking, the laundry, the housework.

Only at his funeral service did friends learn of the earlier years of Pat's life. He had been married before, when he was twenty, but his young wife died when they had been married for only a year. Friends did not know that Pat had come through even darker times when he was younger still. Pat came from a family of eight children. Their father worked in the gas-works, and in the wartime he was in Air Raid Precautions, the ARP, taking his turn at guarding the gas-works at night. One night, Mr Hamilton had changed shifts to oblige a workmate who wanted to be off-duty on a different night, so he was at home. During the night a bomb struck their building. Five of the family were killed: Mr Hamilton and four children, Thomas, Bobby, Jim and Agnes. Mrs Hamilton and the four other children, Hughie, Pat, John and Margaret, were buried in the rubble from the Friday until they were brought out on the Sunday. They were all seriously injured but they survived. Pat's left arm was so badly hurt it was thought he would lose it. But a doctor said they must give it a chance, and Pat kept his arm. It was always weak but he never remarked on it and he lived a full working life.

From what they already knew of him, people thought well of him. Pat was an admirable man, quiet, mannerly, kind, a working man who took wonderful care of his ailing wife. But even those who knew him well had had no hint of the wounds of war which he had carried for more than sixty years. There was a dimension to his life of which people were utterly unaware. The retired railwayman carrying his groceries home in plastic shopping bags was a hero, unacknowledged and silent.

This scene is enacted in communities across Scotland and across other countries, as men and women who have played their part in the drama of war have learned to carry that experience as if it had never been.

THE BOER WAR AND THE GREAT WAR

From time to time in the 1970s, in my early days as a minister, I found myself taking funeral services of men aged about ninety who had fought in the Boer War. I overheard one undertaker saying to another, 'Aye, these old ones are all going now.' Soon they were indeed all gone. I realised that I had been in the company of people who in their younger years had turned the pages of history, and that their experiences were now gone for ever, lost 'like tears in the rain'.

I turned my attention to the generation who had fought in the First World War, the Great War. I enjoyed speaking to them, and enquiring about their memories, seeing through their eyes the momentous events in which they had shared so long before. I found myself wondering if new generations might be able to learn from their thoughts.

REMEMBRANCE SUNDAY

As the minister of a Church of Scotland parish, with many in the congregation who had lived through the Second World War, I had an annual responsibility to hold a special service on Remembrance Sunday. It was a tradition that the members of the uniformed youth organisations, the Boys' Brigade, the Guides and Brownies and Rainbows, would parade on that day with colours flying. I saw that my interest in the lives of these now elderly people might connect with the boys and girls on Remembrance Sunday.

One autumn day, when talking with John Turner, a resident in a local home for the elderly, I asked him if I might try something new. 'Would you let me interview you?' I enquired. 'I'd like to ask you some questions, and then I'd like to tell your answers to the young ones in the church service this coming Remembrance Sunday.' Mr Turner consented. And so began this series of interviews with people from the ordinary life of Castlemilk. People from this large housing scheme on Glasgow's south side, the area to which in the 1950s the local authority moved the population of Glasgow's legendary Gorbals, have given their experiences of war and peace, their reflections on good and evil, poverty and wealth, faith and doubt.

Through these interviews we encounter a tiny fragment of that dialogue which continues without pause within the human community. Ordinary people wrestle constantly with the huge themes of existence. They discuss them and reflect upon them, but their voices are seldom heard beyond the confines of their own living-room or their local public house.

Most reflections on the manner in which war affects human affairs are written by those who have held command. Here, however, are front-line experiences and insights of the rank and file, and the wartime lives of working-class men and women on the home front. In these pages their courage and their clarity of vision speak for themselves.

1985

Mr John Turner

- Mikhail Gorbachev becomes Soviet leader at the age of fifty-four.
- Forty soccer fans die at Bradford City's football ground when the stand goes on fire.
- Forty-one people die in Heysel Stadium, Brussels, when a riot breaks out during a European Cup game.
- Bob Geldof organises the Live Aid Concert in Wembley Stadium.
- Unseeded tennis player Boris Becker wins Wimbledon title at the age of seventeen.
- The wreck of the *Titanic* is found on the bed of the Atlantic Ocean.

In 1985, Mr John Turner, born in Hawick in 1895, is a resident in Glenwood Lodge, a home for the elderly in Castlemilk Drive.

CHILDHOOD IN HAWICK

I left school in 1909, aged fourteen, but there was no work in Hawick. I used to deliver papers and the milk. But I couldn't get a job. I remember that they had closed one of the mills and there must have been hundreds out of work. Then they started a water project and gave people jobs. I remember that some of the office workers got jobs on that and how their hands got all sore from using the pick and shovel. In the end, when I was about sixteen, I got work in a tweed warehouse. Eighteen shillings [*90 pence*] a week I got for that.

WAR BEGINS

When I was twenty, war broke out. About a month after that I went to join up. I went in to Galashiels and they asked what we wanted to join and I said the Gordon Highlanders. So I had to go up to Aberdeen. There were hundreds of us joining up there. One day they lined us all up and they called out our numbers and they told us we were 'Privates'. A shilling we got for joining up and then a shilling a day: the King's Shilling. Then, next day, we got a meal and then a train down to Aldershot where they taught us the ins and outs of soldiering. The first night we were there, there was a big, broad road and then a big expanse of grass. We just slept on the grass because the barracks were full. The second night, they got tents for us and we slept ten to a tent. There was about half-a-dozen of us from Hawick: some from Buccleuch, some from Drumlanrig School; I was at Wilton. We all lived in Hawick. One chap, Charters, lived upstairs from us. He was a fine lad, played rugby for Hawick. He was killed. I'm the only one left. We all joined up the same day. We were in several places camping before we left for France early in 1915. 'Kitchener's Army' they called you. They moved us to Midhurst. There was so many soldiers that two Companies were in private digs but we were in a big hall. They gave us a lot of drill and such like. We shifted from there to Cirencester for three months. There was more drill and then they gave us out our uniforms, kilts and all that. I lost my kilt in the end, some people always kept theirs. But mine was riddled with bullets and soaked in blood and I lost it. My mother died when we were there; she was only forty. She took a heart attack in the night. They told me she had been listening to a band the night before, playing the tattoo. I got home for three days for the funeral.

FRANCE

From Cirencester we went to Rushmoor Camp, I think it was, for about a month, and then to France. We spent the first night in tents near Boulogne. We were only there a day and a half when we got the train on to Calais. Then we got another train away up to Belgium, to near Bethune.

You could see the flashes of the guns firing at night. We arrived in Newly Means [*Noeux-les-Mines*], near there anyway. The Colonel was the first man to be killed. He was an old man, a right sort of toff one. He went up to see the trenches we were to take over. On his way back, a shell landed near him and he was killed. It took us all quite by surprise. They had a military funeral for him but I had got the job of batman to an officer and I was busy so never went.

We took over a section of trenches in the Loos sector. Right away, at night we had things to do: I helped to put out the barbed wire. Then the Battle of Loos came on. I came through all right but the Battalion, fresh men from Scotland, were a greatly reduced number. That was the first time I saw anyone killed. And you got terribly tired. In the trenches there were what you called funk holes, and I used to squeeze in there for a doze.

We got so small in number, with all the men killed and wounded, that they had to join two Battalions together to form one. The Eighth-Tenth Battalion, they called it. After the battle was over, and things settled down, both the German and the British had mines planted. When they went off, if you happened to be near, you thought it was an earthquake. It all went up in the air, chalk, it was, too, all white.

WOUNDED

After a month in the trenches after the battle of Loos, I got wounded for the first time. I was in a nest-shaped part of the trench, and a pathway ran down to the dug-out, which was a sort of built thing. We had to take turns up in that nest, two hours at a time. I got wounded in the hand and leg. My hand, and all the fingers were covered with holes. I was sent off to the hospital at Yeeps [*Ypres*]. While I was there, I had had an aluminium ring on this finger – the Frenchies made them – and my finger had swelled all round it. There was a nurse who tried everything to help me get it off. Eventually with hot water and Vaseline, she got it off but I thought I was going to pass out. I was down there when the Battle of the Somme started.

I got shifted to Eetaps [*Etapes*] for recovery after my wounds. I sat there with a party of men, all different regiments; it was a camp there. We took drills every now and then. I was marked for a draft up the line. They had an inspection. They asked for anyone who had a complaint to take a pace forward. I took the pace forward; I couldn't hold my rifle with my left hand, which had been wounded. The officer sent me to the medical officer. There was this big tent and I saw the doctor. He twisted my fingers and my hand so much that I had to go outside and lie down on the ground. And I wasn't fit to go up the line. But three weeks after that – I had no pals of my own and that sort of thing, all the men coming from different regiments – I went and saw the sergeant and volunteered to go up the line. The sergeant said, unbelieving, like, 'You want to go up the line?' 'Yes', I said. All the men on the base used to play cards, 'Banker' I think it was. And I got fed up with that: some made money, others didn't. I wanted away from it. Going up the line seemed a lot better.

BACK TO THE FRONT: WOUNDED AGAIN

It came the next draft. We got the train up near the Somme and had to sleep out in the open, on the grass or anywhere. We had the job of taking the ammunition up the front line, and we drilled when we got the chance. Making practice attacks, jumping over trenches, bayonet fighting, and all that sort of stuff.

The time came when we'd go up the line. We went through a place, 'Happy Valley' they called it, into the trenches. On the second or third day we got issued with rum. And we were told we'd be going over the top in the afternoon.

The afternoon came, and sure enough we got the order to go over the top. About 100 yards out over the top, we got the order to go half-left. So we switched direction, and I got caught in machine-gun fire; wounded in the leg. I lay there for quite a while. Then trying to crawl back to the lines, I threw away my rifle, haversack, everything, and crawled back. I remember shells coming over, bursting twenty yards behind me, showering me with everything. After a while, maybe an hour, I had managed to get back. When I reached the bit of the trench that jutted out, I went in head first and fell right in. I was back. I sat there for a long time; no-one ever came near me.

I attended to my own wounds; took the bandage out of my pocket, bandaged my leg tight to soak the bleeding. I sat there on the first step, that the men used to stand on when they were firing over the top. I smelt a funny smell as I sat there. I looked down and there was a foot. A German's foot was showing through the bottom of the trench: the body must all have been covered in the trench wall. Another chap by this time was sitting opposite me. Another shell burst and showered us, and he was wounded in the knee. Blood was spurting out of his leg. I helped him to bandage it up and told him to get away as quick as possible to the dressing station.

Night came and I still wasn't moved. I lay down in the bottom of the trench, stuck at the back of the firing step. It was pit-black and I fell asleep. I was wakened by soldiers rushing up the trench; they were stepping on top of me. I shouted, 'Keep to your left! Wounded Man!' but they kept on running and kept stepping on top of me.

THE LONG JOURNEY HOME

In the morning, three officers – who had spoken to me the night before and had asked me why I was sitting there; I said, 'I am wounded, waiting for a stretcher-bearer' – they spotted me again in the morning. 'Talk about serving King and Country,' I said, 'I can't get anyone to help me at all.'

They detailed a man to help me past the barbed wire and over into the next set of trenches. As I went down through that trench, I came on four men all on their hands and knees. I said, 'Excuse me, can I get past?' They never moved. I found they were all dead. They must have gone down on their hands and knees to shield themselves from the wind, the blast, from an exploding shell; but it had got them anyway. I had to walk over the top of them.

Then I saw two stretcher-bearers, and they decided to take me back to the dug-out. I lay there among a group of men, lying there wounded and waiting to be attended to. I lay there a long time before I was attended to. There was a German wounded man lying next to me. We were both wanting water, but there wasn't any. Eventually they found an ambulance for some of us and I was sent to Abbeville. I was a while there: it was a huge hospital sort of a place, with big marquees full of wounded soldiers. It was in the summer time and the sides of the tents were lifted up. You saw them passing, carrying the dead soldiers away to be buried somewhere. After I had been there a while they said, 'Would you like to get home?' I said, 'I widnae half.' I was taken away down on the canal then on to a train, then to Le Havre, and the boat.

I was on the top deck of the boat and I couldn't sleep very well lying up there. It was the *Esturias*, a big boat, I think they called it that, the *Esturias*. As we came to England there was an air raid on and we had to stop off the Isle of Wight till it was all clear.

Well, we landed home. I was put on an ambulance train and taken to Birmingham. Then they sent me to Ireland to see if they could put my leg and foot right because I couldn't move my foot. It just dropped whenever I tried to move it. They gave me massage and electricity treatment. It never did mend. I got a pension of thirty shillings [£1.50] a week for a few months and then it got reduced and, after a few years, I signed some piece of paper, got some money from them, and the pension stopped. But my foot has always been like that. And I don't know how I've managed really. For I even used to go cycling with my youngest boy, down to Troon and Largs and the like. And all that leg could do was get the pedal round far enough for the good leg to do all the work.

And when I did get back to work, I was a tailor's cutter; they used to pay my wages, but less what I was getting in that pension.

Anyway, after that time in Ireland they sent me back to Aberdeen. And I went through lots of drill there. They wanted to send me back to the Front. Colonel Butt passed me fit – but I had to go into hospital again for another operation on my leg. Colonel Butt was one of that sort. I remember one man who walked with two crutches and his feet were very swollen and Colonel Butt said he was putting it on and passed him fit and sent him back to the Front.

But that was my war over and I went down to Glasgow looking for work.

GOODNESS IN UNEXPECTED PLACES

It was a terrible time, all that. And you felt that it wasn't necessary. They could have sorted it out by discussions and never had to go to war at all. I don't know how I got through it that time I was wounded. But I never thought about dying; I never thought, 'I might die.' I suppose I was young and all that. But I'm likely the only one of us that joined up from Hawick that time. There was Charters and Marshall, they were both killed. There was Blair, he was an older man than me; he came though all right but I doubt if he's still living. Mann, there was; he died of wounds. There was Miller; and Anderson, he was a printer; they were both killed. I think I'll be the only one left. I remember the first Armistice Parade, after the war ended. I wanted to go on that, on the Parade. But I never went. I've never been on any of those things for the old soldiers and that. But I think about them all.

You saw such bad things but you saw so many good things too. Just ordinary men, but so good. I remember a man, he was an older man, must have been thirty-five or forty, older than us. He used to look after me in the trenches, see that I knew how to take care of myself, see that I was all right. A big, coarse man, that not everyone would take to. He could drink a bit, and things like that. But a good man.

I couldn't come and talk at your service myself. I've had this cold for weeks. But I'll be glad if you think that there's anything in that you could tell them.

———— ‹‹✺›› ————

John Turner spent his entire working life as a tailor. He married and he and his wife had two sons. Although he lived in Glasgow for the rest of his life, he retained the

directness and honesty of his Hawick upbringing. He and his wife moved together into Glenwood Lodge, one of Castlemilk's homes for the elderly. After Mrs Turner's death, John lived on in Glenwood Lodge comfortably, until his own death in 1989 at the age of ninety-four.

1986

Mr George Godfrey

- Iran captures the Iraqi oil port of Faw near Basra, destroying 570 Iraqi tanks and capturing 140.
- The United States launches air strikes against Libya, using bombers based in Britain.
- The nuclear reactor in Chernobyl goes on fire in the world's worst civil nuclear disaster.
- Maradona's 'Hand of God' helps Argentina to victory in the World Cup soccer tournament.
- Sir Robert Armstrong, Cabinet Secretary, apologises to an Australian court for being 'economical with the truth' about spy Peter Wright's book.

In 1986, George Godfrey is a retired baker. He and his wife have two daughters. They have lived in Castlemilk since the housing scheme was built in 1955.

⎯⎯⎯«◉»⎯⎯⎯

BORN TO WAR

I was born in the house in Govanhill Street on Hallowe'en. The 31st October 1915. My father was away in the war at the time. When the news was given to him, my father was actually standing in the trenches in the Dardanelles. They were in action at the time and his gun was red hot.

There were so many of my family in the forces you'd need the Kelvin Hall to hold them all. My father had six brothers. My mother was one of thirteen and her brothers all fought in that war: big strong men they were. One of them was gassed.

I left school at fourteen; Victoria Primary, then Calder Street Secondary. I had too much football in my head to do well at the academic stuff; I got prizes for my handwriting though. But it was football. When I see a ball even now, my feet are itching. I've still got a pair of football boots, they were sent out to me when I was in the army in Italy during the war. Really old-fashioned, block toes; and the shin-guards: the family say they should be in the museum. I played outside right. Jim Wilkie's dad and I were mates: he got signed by Ashfield, and they were looking at me too. But that was all. I was on the verge of Junior football, as we called it. When I left school I was a message boy, and then I went into a bakery, just off Allison Street.

WAR AND FAMILY LIFE

When the war broke out I didn't join up at once; I kept on at my work. Why didn't I join up at once, volunteer? Well. Even when I did join up in 1941, the worst spot was saying goodbye to my mother ... I can see her yet ... On the landing ...

I joined the South Lancashire Regiment first, and went down to Warrington Barracks. They were forming the Army Catering Corps. They knew that fighting men need good food and getting a baker was a good thing.

And round about this time Elizabeth and I had been going to get married. But with me being called up we finally got married on Hogmanay 1941, in my mother-in-law's house in Ruby Crescent, Motherwell. I was on fourteen days' leave, which they told me during it I was to count as embarkation leave. Then I had forty-eight hours' leave in March, and then a week in May. And then, after that, we didn't see each other for three years and three months. Elizabeth was working in service all that time.

OFF TO THE WAR

We went by ship overseas in 1942. We even anchored off Largs and I could see the big house where Elizabeth worked, but I couldn't get to see her. They found out that she was there, and after that they wouldn't even let me up on deck. Thinking I'd make a run for it, no doubt.

We sailed south to Durban and then up the Red Sea to Egypt where we joined the Eighth Army. The Eighth Army had won in North Africa and we went up northwards through Jerusalem and Hebron and did a lot of heavy training in the Lebanon.

From Egypt, we sailed to Malta and then to Sicily. We went into Sicily the day after the Invasion began, Day plus One. That was where I saw what war was really like. We just landed on a beach, there was no facilities for bringing in a boat. We set up our field kitchen and cooked up a lot of tinned stuff. By now I had been attached to the Royal Engineers and I was with a unique mob, the 13th Field Survey Company of the Royal Engineers. We had two complete mobile printing presses for map-making and there was another party that calibrated the guns. So while it was not an actual fighting unit, you worked with the gunners in the field and you were right up at the front. And that place in Sicily where we landed, the smell of death was in the place. All the ambulances with the people inside ... I used to feel numb, as if your brain had ceased to work. My belief in God got a severe dunt, I can tell you. From Sicily to the end of the war, there was a host of things happened, a man is bound to change. The war just finished in time for me.

WAR AND PERSONAL FAITH

I had always been a church-goer. I was baptised as an adult at seventeen. I used to go every Sunday to the Hermon Baptist Church. I sang in the choir, it was just opposite the end of Aikenhead Road. But in those days in Sicily I found that I had left all my religious thoughts and habits behind in Govanhill. Then I gradually came back to all these things as the story unfolded.

My own turning point came in Italy. We'd just moved up to this place, above Naples, a wee tiny village. The Germans were retreating. We set up the kitchen, of all places, in the village cemetery. I went off for a walk round the village. I came up a wee path and I turned left into this new part. There was green, green grass, the like of grass you just didn't see in Italy, maybe a stretch twenty yards long. And there were little white crosses, sixteen or eighteen young soldiers buried there. When I started reading the names, I had to turn and go away. I didn't know any of them. I was a stranger. But I read their names and their ages, eighteen, nineteen, eighteen; they came from Rutherglen and from Glasgow. When I turned away, I thought of their parents; their hopes and ambitions; cut down. Everybody's got their own thoughts; a lot of chaps maybe never cared much about things. But that's like any nation at war; everything coarsens, doesn't it? Yes, that war just finished in time for me.

PEACE

The day war finished, I was in Athens. There was this kind of amphitheatre; I was walking about and I stopped to have a cigarette. Someone said, 'The war's finished!' There was a silence and I just sat there; then it broke over you. That it was finished. It was marvellous ...

REMEMBRANCE

And Remembrance Day. Yes, even during the war, I used to think of Remembrance Day. If your CO was interested in that, he would arrange a special parade for everyone. But I thought about it anyway. I used to think about the earlier war, the 1914–18 war. I used to think of the conditions they had had to suffer, my father being a machine gunner in the trenches. We thought things were bad for us, but it was so much worse for them. Yes, Remembrance Day, even in the war, I remembered it, very much so.

And now, on Remembrance Sunday, I would say I think about it all, but especially about four or five outstanding people. I keep in touch with two friends I was with in the Army. I think of them. One of my close friends was lost. Jim Anderson, he stayed up the same street, 31 Govanhill Street. He was coming out to be a dentist. He was in the Air Force, and he was killed in a raid. I never did hear exactly what happened because they moved away. I think of him.

I was home on leave, after the end of the war in Europe. And that was when I heard of the bombing of Hiroshima. That was frightening to say the least. At first you thought, 'Good. The war's over.' But as time goes on you start putting the facts together. I've no doubt in my mind there's people would use it if we didn't have it; but there's always a dread in you.

The war kept George Godfrey away from home for three years and three months. The harsh memories of war never left him. But he enjoyed his life, and he was an ardent fan of Glasgow Rangers football team. Even in his old age a football at his feet could bring out some of his earlier skills. His working life was spent as a baker. Starting each morning at three o'clock – two o'clock on Saturdays – he worked with A. & T. Scott in Battlefield, making morning rolls and bread for over thirty years until his retirement. He and his wife, Elizabeth, had two daughters, then a grandson and grand-daughter. The family was part of the local parish church; George variously a Sunday School teacher, in the choir, an Elder and the Deputy Session Clerk. Mrs Godfrey contracted cancer and had to undergo a radical amputation of her leg, losing half her pelvis. But for the next twenty-five years she lived as if her condition was nothing out of the ordinary. Similarly, when George developed Parkinson's disease the two of them took that, too, in their stride. George died at home very peacefully in 1992 at the age of seventy-six.

1987

Mrs Mary Keenan

- Terry Waite, envoy of the Archbishop of Canterbury, is kidnapped in Beirut.
- The *Herald of Free Enterprise*, a cross-Channel ferry, capsizes with the loss of over 200 lives.
- The Duchess of Windsor's jewellery is sold for £31,380,197.
- The Tories are elected for a third consecutive term, with Mrs Thatcher as Prime Minister, with a majority of over 100.
- The 'storm of the century' lashes England, after weather forecasts fail to give warning.
- An IRA bomb explodes at the Enniskillen Remembrance Day parade.
- President Reagan of the USA and Soviet leader Mikhail Gorbachev sign first-ever treaty to cut the number of nuclear war-heads.

In 1987, Mrs Mary Keenan is over ninety, small in stature, with bright eyes and a great sense of fun. She is always on the move, out visiting friends or family.

THE OUTBREAK OF THE FIRST WORLD WAR

I remember the day war was declared in 1914. I had been over in Ireland staying with friends and I came home from Belfast that Sunday morning. And war was declared. We never thought for a minute it was going to last so long.

THE FAMILY

I was born in Cathcart Street in 1896. They've changed it all now. It ran between Paisley Road and Scotland Street. There was eight of us in the family altogether, and I was the second oldest. My mother was quite strict you know, quite abrupt. Still, everybody ran for her. They would run for Granny Bell. If they weren't well: 'What do you think this is?', 'What do you think that is?' They would always run for her.

She made us say our prayers and grace before your meat. We used to go to the wee Mission Hall in Cathcart Street. With the Foundry Boys and the Penny Bank and all that. It was the Mission of the Pollok Street United Free Church. And we used to go to Sunday School. And then there was the trips. There was the Maxwell Church trip. At the school the teacher would ask, 'Hands up all those that are going on the Maxwell trip?' and the hands would all go up. You would get marched from Pollok Street at nine in the morning down to the Kingston Dock, with your tinny round your neck and then all day on the boat to Port Bannatyne or somewhere. And you'd come back looking like beetroots. And there was Paddy Black's trip too, with the horses.

In the war, my father was a cook in the boats and in the Navy. My sister, Nan, was a nurse – though she didn't go abroad; and my brother, John, was in the Suffolk Hussars as a despatch rider, and he was mostly in Cork in Ireland.

WAR BRINGS A CHANGE OF WORK

At the start of the war, I was in tailoring at the corner of Mitchell Street. I was doing lapels, for only coppers, half a crown a week; is that twelve pence in today's money? I got fed up with that; and Lizzie Malone, that came from Uddingston, she was joining up for munitions, and so of course I went with her and we got taken out to Bishopton. But I wasn't there for very long. There was an explosion and we had to get away. I remember it. There was a big bang and we all ran. So they moved us away from there. I got into McKee and Baxters, an engineering shop in Copland Road. It was a fortnight night-shift and a fortnight day-shift, from six a.m. in the morning. You had to work in those days. But the wages were much better than the tailoring.

In McKee and Baxters I was a turner. I worked in one of the engineering bays and I had a machine to watch. It put the screw on a part, not a very big part, for the marine engines. I remember I got my ears bored there, too, on the night shift. It was your mates that would do it, with a needle in a piece of cork. I remember telling my mother when I got home. 'You'd no right getting your ears bored!'

But there was better wages there than at the tailoring, and the jobs were there because the men were all away at the war.

THE FIRST ARMISTICE

It was some day, the Armistice. What a day! Everybody was going daft, dancing in the street. It was wonderful.

MARRIAGE TO BOB

When the war was finished, I went back to tailoring: to Charlie Dowden's in Carlton Place, just a wee bit by the suspension bridge, and I was there until such time as I got married.

My husband, Bob, was in the war, in the Inniskillen Dragoons, the Irish Rifles. I didn't know him then, though. I knew his father and his brother before I ever knew him. Bob was wounded in France. A shell burst and his back got it: you could put your hand in his lung. And there was as many bits of shrapnel. But they couldn't operate. He was well known in the Victoria Infirmary as the 'Iron Man' because of all the shrapnel! He was a great big strapping man – and his mother had seventeen of a family and she was just a wee woman, too.

Bob didn't want me to work. He was a steel erector, doing jobs all over the country. So I used to go with him.

He was down in Chepstow in Wales, taking down the cranes from the First War to build them up in Wellington Quay to get them ready for the next war. He worked with Arrolls' and then with Redpath Brown. And he was in the hangars too, building hangars for the aircraft for the Second War. He used to be away for eighteen months at a time, all over England with Redpath Brown.

You could near enough say that it was the wars that gave him his livelihood. He was a grafter – a terrible man for work. There was a time, of course, that there wasn't work, and he would maybe get only one or two days' work a week. But he never drew Burroo money. Then there was a girder fell on him at the Whifflet, Cambuslang, and they sent him out of the hospital in a plaster jacket. And he was three years off with his spine. And then he was back to work. He was a grafter. He was always getting injured at his work: I don't think he had an inch in his head but what was stitched.

DIFFERENCE BETWEEN FIRST WAR AND SECOND WAR

But the Second War was that different from the First War. You saw the war in the Second War. Before the Second War, I used to go away with Bob. He would be away building the hangars and I'd shut up the house and go away with him and stay in the Digs. We were staying in Bury St Edmunds when the Second War broke out: John Street, Bury St Edmunds.

Then later on in the war, Bob was working in Liverpool with Redpath Brown again, working building cranes at the docks. And Liverpool was bombed. Terrible it was. You saw the splashes of blood on the walls. Terrible. Well, Bob didn't want me there with all that going on so he chased me home. And the night I got home to Glasgow was the night they bombed Clydebank. And in the Second War it was as bad at home. I remember the Co-operative got bombed at the docks. And a tram in Nelson Street was hit. One of my mates, her daughter was in it. And I remember walking down to my mother's one morning after the Blitz, walking along the top of big piles of rubble, all the buildings down. And there was a lot of French sailors killed that night too.

REMEMBRANCE DAY

On Remembrance Day, I think about everybody, all the men that were killed. I don't really think of the Germans. It was just like a job and they have to do it, wasn't it? If they didn't go and shoot, they'd be shot. You thought bad of the Germans at the time; but there's no hate now. Remembrance Day always brings back sad memories. I used always to go to George Square on Remembrance Sunday, to the Service, every year. But not now. I used to go with a friend. Cissie Cobb's man was killed in the First War, and her two brothers, too. I used to go along with her, just to be with her there.

WAR AND THOUGHTS OF GOD

When we heard about the first atom bomb, we never thought that much about it; we just thought, well that's the end of the war. Though you wonder now where it's all going to finish, don't you?

But that's the only time there's plenty of work, when there's a war, isn't it? That's the worst of it. And it's the innocent that get hurt so often.

When you think about war, why there's all these wars, you wonder at times what God was thinking. And then you think on yourself, and think that maybe it's all the punishing we're getting for all the badness we do. There's too much badness going on in the world: maybe God thinks we need a clip on the ear.

But I've always gone to church except when I was staying in England, and I've always believed in God. I always say my prayers and I try to think about others. I pray every night for all them that's departed and all my friends, and others that I don't know. And I thank God for getting me to be this age; and ask him to keep me safe till tomorrow – sort of style. And I try to do what I can for anybody.

And as for me, I wouldn't like to be a burden to anybody. But you'll not go before your time; and we've all got our own ways to go, haven't we?

Mary Keenan died just before Christmas 1988, at the age of ninety-two. She died only twenty-four hours after being taken ill when out as usual with her friends at the Bingo. She was born in Cathcart Street, Glasgow. Though she and her husband, Bob, had no children of their own they were favourites throughout the family. With Bob's work taking him all over the country, Mary would shut up their house in Carnoustie Street and go with him and look after him. At other times she worked at the tailoring, and as a cleaner on the boats which came in to Glasgow's docks. Mary was a much-loved aunt and great-aunt, who travelled to visit members of the family circle in Australia and America. Vigorous to the very end of her life, she went several times a week to visit two brothers still in Glasgow, taking them flasks of her home-made soup.

1988

Mr William Allison

- Three members of the IRA are gunned down in Gibraltar by British SAS soldiers in civilian clothing.
- At Milltown cemetery, Belfast, a Loyalist gunman opens fire indiscriminately and throws grenades among mourners at the funeral of the three IRA dead.
- A disastrous fire on North Sea oil platform Piper Alpha kills 167 men.
- A US missile shoots down an Iranian airliner over the Gulf; all 286 people on board are killed.
- Ben Johnson is stripped of his Olympic Gold Medal and 100 metres world record after testing positive for banned drugs.
- George Bush wins US Presidential election.
- Pan Am flight 103 explodes over the Scottish town of Lockerbie.

In 1988, Bill Allison is a sixty-two-year-old bricklayer with the Glasgow District Council. On some days his basic pay is increased by five pence an hour when, slung in a cradle, he hangs down the outside of the multi-storey flats, re-pointing the windows.

WHY DO YOUNG MEN JOIN THE FORCES?

There's things I always do remember around this time of the year.

I volunteered for the Navy for two reasons, really. The first was that I'd always wanted to go to sea. And then, secondly, when I left school I had a crowd of pals and I was the youngest. And they were all getting called up. So I went and volunteered. I was working as an apprentice bricklayer at the time. My father had died when I was just nine; he was only twenty-nine. I was left the oldest of five, then. My mother married again a few years later, and I became the oldest of eight; seven boys and a sister. Only one of the brothers never went into the forces. Six of us served in the Forces at one time or another. With my father dead, my grandmother had always told me, 'You'll be a bricklayer like your grandfather.' So when I left school my grandfather got me a job as an apprentice bricklayer. And that's why I'm a bricklayer yet.

I was serving my time, my third year, with Cowiesons of Charles Street. I didn't have to join up, they said. They could get me deferred. But I wanted to volunteer. I remember the boss saying, though, 'Away you go son. I was the same as you in the First War.' So that was me away.

It was Moffat Street we used to live, it used to be called South York Street, just opposite the graveyard. I was in the BB when I was a boy – the 89th attached to Shearer Memorial Church. I was three years in the Lifeboys, and two years in the Company Section. And we met every week in the Drill Hall in Butterbiggins Road. It was a smart crowd there. There were no games at that time on a BB night. It was drill, marching, drill and more drill. I wasn't really keen on this marching carry-on. But when it came to the Navy I found I knew all the drills. So any occasion that came up, I was always picked for it! We had a Pipe Band in the 89th. I remember I was learning the pipes. Then this night at home my younger brother pokered the fire with my chanter and that was that! I never went back; too scared. They came to the door for me, right enough, two or three times. But I was hiding behind the door!

PATROL SERVICES, FAREHAM

When I joined the Navy I was sent to Patrol Services, MTBs, Motor Launches; I was an anti-aircraft gunner on patrols off the south coast of England. At the latter end of my time there you used to feel sorry when those doodle-bugs came over: a plane with a light on the end.

When you watched the light go out you would say to yourself, 'There's some poor soul going to cop it now.' When the light went out, that was it: there was a bang.

When we were on patrol duties, we were based on shore and we were in an army barracks, a sort of training camp in a place called Fareham, outside Portsmouth. Every Remembrance Day, I remember the guys that were killed next door to me there. At night you would hear planes coming in. In the dark you couldn't tell who they were, so they used to drop flares, blue, green, yellow, various colours. And you'd know the colours as they came in; and that was how you identified them then; you knew it was one of ours. Well, apparently, what I'm led to believe, the Air Force had been bombing Germany, and they came in, back home again; and one guy tagged on behind them and came in and dropped a bomb on the barracks there. I was blown out of my bed. The feeling I got was just that the whole bunk bed had risen up into the air. Well, we came out and this hut next to us had been bombed. Every one of them was killed; must have been about twenty or thirty guys killed.

I always think in my mind of one young fellow, coming out to be a naval officer, a nice, clean-looking boy, eighteen or nineteen – we were all just round about that age – he had blond hair. I don't remember him by name, but it's just when you're doing your training, and you're washing up and that. A right cheery guy he was, always saying, 'Hello, how are you doing?' and that. That night, he bled to death. In the Navy you were always doing things at the double; we were always doubling across the Parade Ground. That night, he was carried across the Parade ground. 'No need to double across it tonight,' he said. I don't think he knew he was dying; both his legs were off. He died; yes, he died. They called for volunteers then and we had to clear everything up. Complete confusion there was. I was one of the funeral party at the graveside later, there. And there was different relatives there. And there was one girl. To this day I can see her face yet, how she was, a young girl; maybe her husband, her boyfriend, in the communal grave. These things stick in my mind every year. Not the date, but that particular occasion, when all those boys were killed. I feel it was a waste of life. Boys of eighteen, nineteen years of age. I never knew them, so many of them, but I remember them on Remembrance Day.

JAPAN: HIROSHIMA

I think, too, on Japan. After being on that patrol work, I was sent off to join another ship in Liverpool. A huge ship it was, with two huge doors in the side. It was like walking into a factory, like a vast factory. It was a troop ship, with room for about 2,000 men. And after we took troops on at Greenock, we sailed for the Far East.

You see, you didn't know where you were going all the time. You get on a boat; they don't tell you where you are going. They just shove you in this boat and that's it; 'You're going.' And when you get there, then you know where you are, then. We put troops ashore in Bombay and while we were there it was VJ Day, the end of the war in Japan. Then we put troops off in Batavia, then in Hong Kong, and then we went to Japan, a place called Kure, the port about an hour from Hiroshima, where the bomb had been dropped two weeks before. A funny thing, a pal from the next close to where I lived was standing there on the dockside in Kure: one of the Redcaps directing the troops.

We went on the train from Kure to Hiroshima; people all got up to give you a seat. Women got up to give you a seat. You were the 'masters', kind of style, you know. I didn't agree with that. Bowing away; everybody bowing to you; young and old bowed away; you were the masters, you'd beat them. It was embarrassing, as if you were a great power – you werenae.

Hiroshima itself was just like a big desert. A few buildings were still standing here and there. There was a big steel beam, like a burnt match. You felt as if, if you just touched it, it would have gone over. People were still living there, down under the ground, in pits, just covered with tarpaulin. Women and children. You felt sorry for the kids, the people who were living there. Although they were Japanese, you still felt – I did anyway – I felt sorry for them, you know. You felt it wasn't really their fault, they were just human beings the same as anybody else. Take the average man in the world, black, yellow, white; working people, just working-class people. They don't want to go and fight somebody else. I think war's caused by pure greed; greed for money, power. And unfortunately, we're the guys who do the dirty work. Every Remembrance Sunday my mind's on these things. You say, 'What is it for? What is it worth?'

In Hiroshima, the thing that sticks in my mind is that huge steel beam, like a burnt matchstick. Steel burnt like a match, completely burnt to a cinder, still standing. If you'd touched it, it would've gone over.

We'd heard about the bomb but you didn't realise at the time. When I saw Hiroshima, I can't say I was frightened, more a kind of sorrow, seeing the state people were living in, the poverty, and all that. You couldn't see the streets. There weren't streets. Just like a desert. You couldn't say, 'Go to so and so street', because there weren't streets anymore. Just stalls among the ruins, like the Barras, temporary stalls, selling goods. I'd like to go back and see it; they say it's a marvellous city now.

It didn't strike you at the particular time that it was something quite different, this bomb. You knew the war was over and you hoped you'd get home sometime, now. You just thought in your mind, 'That's some mess. That was some bomb, that; that could cause that damage.' You didn't realise at the time. In later years, as you get older, you think, 'That was some blooming bomb.' And it's nothing, nowadays, compared with what they've got. It's a frightening thing. Just one of them, these big ones now, and that's it. You don't need to bother with a new roof for your church then; you can forget about it! Just needs one idiot to press the button, do the wrong thing there, and that's humanity gone, isn't it? So I don't know if it was a good thing or a bad thing. It was a good thing, because it stopped the war, it did save a lot of lives there, no doubt. But it destroyed a lot of lives. And no doubt in the future it will destroy more lives. They keep experimenting with these things, too; all in the name of science.

MINES AND PRAYERS

But you were relieved that the war was over, and that you'd come out of it all right. You had a lot of silent prayers yourself – sitting in a boat as you go over a minefield. You see an occasional boat hitting a mine and blowing up and you wonder; 'There but for the grace of God go I', more or less. I've seen boats sinking just hitting a mine. Even in the invasion of France, D-Day, this boat had just dropped troops. It was turning back to England. Hit a mine. No doubt the crew were killed. It hit this mine and just seemed to turn up like a big multi-storey building, and sank. You have no chance with these things. One minute you're there; next minute you're not there. You're just lucky if you survive in the water.

I felt awfully sorry for the soldiers. We loaded them into the landing craft and put them ashore. They'd had a terrible journey on the ship, sea-sick and everything, couldn't eat their meals. Couldn't get a sleep, couldn't get into a hammock, couldn't master it. We were able to manage but the poor soldiers had a terrible life. Then we put them ashore to fight a war. The thing's ridiculous. We never had much church services on our ship. We never had a chaplain on our ship. I don't know if chaplains approve of war, or condone it exactly. They didn't do the actual fighting, I know; but I can't fathom why they should do it. I remember when we went through the Malacca Straights at Singapore. We were the first ship to go through from West to East after the fall of Japan. And it was heavily mined. Every man on deck, lining the rails. I said a few silent prayers then, I don't mind telling you. Very heavily mined. Fortunately we made it; the convoy went right through.

THE FELLOWSHIP OF WAR – AND THE DOUBTS

At the time you don't think of the waste of life in war. War is just part of your life. You make friends, good friends. These were your mates. If it came to it, you'd have died for them; fought for them and died for them. They were your pals, your life on that ship. There were many good things too, you learned discipline, learned how to behave yourself.

And you get to wondering how many of your mates are still living. The oldest man on our ship was twenty-seven. The rest of us were eighteen, nineteen, twenty, twenty-one. It was a shame really, he had hardly any pals; too old. Five years made such a lot of difference.

And I'm glad I've seen those parts of the world. But I'd never go again. I don't feel I'd go and fight for anyone again. I don't know if that's a religious thought or just common sense. But I feel it's maybe a bit of bitterness, seeing the state of the country, people being tramped down. If I was eighteen now, I would join nothing. In the war, it was terrible to be a Conscientious Objector. I think I'd be one now. I couldn't go and fight for anybody, the way people are getting treated nowadays.

STILL LIVING

As I said, you always did have your prayers there in the forces. Your wee silent prayers to yourself, more or less. Most of them probably did. As you went through the dark nights not knowing if anything was going to happen to you, with the mines, and submarines, and various things like that. And when you did, you thanked God you'd come out of it alive. And when I came out of the Navy, I joined the church. Anna and I got married there, in St Margaret's, Polmadie. Most of my life, the church has been part of my life. Apart from those few years after my career in the BB got cut short by that chanter! It didn't suddenly come over my mind, 'I think I'll go to church.' Basically it was always there.

So that's where my thoughts are on Remembrance Day. The guys who got killed. I don't know where they came from, or who they were, or what they were. I never knew whether they were Church of England, Church of Scotland, Roman Catholic or nothing at all. But I remember them.

And here I am. Glad to be, as my friend George Godfrey always says, 'Still living!'

Bill Allison was a bricklayer all his working life. His abilities would have coped well with promotion, but he preferred to stick to the tools and to be on equal terms with his work-mates. He and his wife Anna had two children who have achieved success in their working lives. In the local parish church, Bill carried the responsibilities of Session Clerk, his steady influence valued by everyone. He was a founder of the local inter-Church bowling league, which was instrumental in forming friendships all across the area, notably between Roman Catholic and Protestant members of the community. Bill's retirement from work coincided with Anna's developing Alzheimer's disease, and Bill cared for her day and night. But the strain of it told on him. His GP warned him, anxiously, that Anna must go into care. Bill visited her daily for eighteen months, until he took ill suddenly himself and died at the age of sixty-eight. Anna out-lived him by two years.

1989

Mr Robert Ross

- First woman Anglican Bishop consecrated in the USA.
- Last Soviet troops leave Afghanistan after ten-year occupation.
- Ninety-four people die in Sheffield's Hillsborough stadium.
- The tanks in Beijing's Tiananmen Square are defied by one man, but then hundreds are massacred.
- The Berlin Wall is breached: bulldozers tear open new crossing-points between East and West Germany, and people are permitted to cross freely.
- In Czechoslovakia, the Communist party leader and entire politburo resign. Democracy in prospect.
- The Superpowers declare an end to the Cold War.
- In England, the Water Boards are privatised, ending the free municipal supply of water. Scotland resists the change.

In 1989, Mr Bobby Ross has retired from his working life with the Highways Department. He and his wife Nell keep up a wide range of friendships. One daughter and her family live close at hand, and they regularly visit their other daughter and her family in Canada.

THOUGHTS ON THE FIRST WORLD WAR

My father was in the First War. I remember when he came back on leave. I was only young, then. I was born on 4th January 1913. I was brought up in Swan Street, behind Canal Street, Port Dundas, though I was born in Foundry Place – in the cottages at the back of the foundry – wee cottages, like the miners' rows they were.

I mind my mother knitting socks for the Army: a penny a pair or a ha'penny a pair or something. They supplied her with the wool, but she did all the knitting, working, trying to get enough to keep us. It was a very hard time. She had the four of us – Peggy and John and Bella and me. She had a hard time of it. I remember just at the end of the war getting buns off the troops at the Boatmen's Institute. The soldiers would always give us something. I'd nip into the blacksmith's shop and get some tea. I was always being given horses from the stable to take to the smiddy, and Jimmy there, he'd get me to take horses back for people.

My father came back from the war all right, but his brother, Walter, was killed in the war. And his other brother called his son after him, called him Walter. And that young Walter was blown up on the last day of the Second War. He lost his legs and died of the gangrene. He was taking German prisoners in on the last day of the war. He was a lad who didn't need to go to the Army, either, for he worked with Beardmores and didn't need to go. But he wanted to go and so he joined up. Funny how it was the two with the same name, the two Walters, that died. One in the First War, one in the Second. My father was stationed in Ayr Barracks for a long time, and we went and lived in Ayr for four years.

And my father-in-law, Nell's father, he was in the First War, too. And he was hit with shrapnel: he had this piece of shrapnel in the back of his neck, and it always gave him trouble, right until he died.

KEPT OUT OF THE WAR BY AN ACCIDENT

I wanted to join up at the start of the war in 1939. 'Did the Cameronians not send for you,' they asked me, 'if you were in the Territorials?' I says, 'No', and I told them about my eye, and how I was discharged through the accident. And that was what was printed on my papers – 'Unfit for further service' – through my eye. I'd enlisted as a Territorial in 1931, for five years with the Cameronians. I was in the transport, and in these days it was horses. In the Regular Army, the horses was all trained up before you got them. But we just got them off the contractors. All sorts of backgrounds of horses. And you only got two or three days to get them together. There was stalls for the horses in the Regular Army, but in the Territorials they were just tied to ropes. And you had to feed two horses at a time. And it wasn't as if you had an ordinary feed-bag and you just give it to the horse. You had to stand at the back of the horses with a bag on each shoulder, and the horses were starving, and they're jumping about, and their tails are waggling, and that was what happened. This one hit my eye with its tail. And I never knew how bad it was. And the Medical Officer put the wrong stuff on my eye. Whatever they treated it with it burned my eye, and I was climbing the wall with it. The specialist in the eye hospital said, 'If I could find who did that to your eye I would jail him.' In the end they gave me a small pension for it, but I had all sorts of skin grafts. You'll never guess what the pension was – nine and ninepence [47 pence]. But it was enough to stop them taking me in to the Army again. I thought I would have been going. There was a man went in a fortnight before me, and he had only the one eye, too – a glass eye he had. I did want to join up. Your mates were all going. It put you in a funny position; I was disappointed at the time, quite disappointed. But the war was here in Glasgow itself, too. There was people suffering here, too. The war was in Glasgow.

A WORKING LIFE WITH HORSES

I was at Dobbies' Loan School, and after I left school at fourteen I started out as a stable boy in Hemphills' Stable in James's Street, Port Dundas, where my father was stableman. There was twenty-five horses to muck out and feed. Seven days a week you did it, running the barrow-loads of muck up the plank on to the dung midden, and all for ten shillings [50 pence] a week. Then I went on to be a light larry boy, a light carter. You just had light horse, a horse of fifteen hands – we called it a pony – not a heavy horse. Then the boss of the Firm, he was killed, old James Hemphill himself, and McMillan of Govanhill took over.

I went on to be second man on the steam wagon, working on the roads. You had to load the wagon, shovelling half-inch chips on to the steamer, and then spreading it from the back of it on to the roads. I worked with one man on those steamers. He was shell-shocked from the First War. He was near enough a vegetable. He was just a bag of nerves. He just daunered about the yard. They told us he was a really smart man before the war. He wasn't old, not fifty. He got a small wage for just helping around the yard, carrying tools and the like. He was just part of that yard with McMillan's of Govanhill. He was a wreck of a man and you felt sorry for him. I felt sorry for him, anyway.

I was still just young when I began working on those steamers. But I complained to McMillan that I wasn't getting the wage I was due, for I was doing a man's work. So I left, and I was barred from the Burroo. And in those days it was the Means Test and my father couldn't afford to keep me, so I went to stay with my brother at Highcraighall Road in the Cowcaddens. And I got a job doing anything I could: carrying the coal, or anything at all. And when things got really bad, I started up on my own. The brother helped me, right enough. He started me out. I started out pushing my hand barrow, with the brickets, selling fish, anything. Then we got a horse and lorry, and at one time we had six horses, and delivered all kinds of goods, mostly grain. Horses are great animals, very friendly animals. For years, day after day at the carting, going as far as Bridge of Weir, I had nothing to talk to but the horse. You got to know your horse, and it would get to know you. You'd always have carrot in your pocket and give it to them. They're living creatures – and the majority of them are friendly animals. I never liked to use a whip on a horse. They know what you are saying, and you can coax them.

ARMISTICE DAY

I remember what it was like every Armistice Day, the 11th of November, when everything used to stop at eleven o'clock. No matter where you were, that day at eleven o'clock everything stopped. And if you were out with your horse and your own lorry you had a kine hanging from the back of the back wheel. At about twenty-to-eleven you'd always have it ready on that particular day. You'd be loaded with two or three ton, and you'd have your kine trailing, a wee block of wood, just sliding along the road at the back of your wheel. And when it came to the time, at exactly eleven o'clock and everything stopped, you stopped, and on the wee bit of hill the kine checked your back wheel and it saved you coming back down the hill. And you'd get off the lorry and talk to your horse, settle it, and stand by its head for the two minutes, and it would stand still.

WARTIME WORK DELIVERING THE GRAIN

The grain trade began to break up with the war, so we sold four of the horses. We kept one; and the brother's boy in England, I gave him a start with the horse and a contract with a foundry. I didn't think I could make a wage enough to keep us now that I was married, so I got a job with McFarlanes' of North Street – the stable was in Cleveden Lane. The grain came in at Queen's dock, Prince's Dock, Meadowside Granary. And I used to deliver it. It was feed I delivered, all the way out as far as Bowling. I used to deliver to a woman in Old Kilpatrick. She kept goats and hens. Feed for horses went to Hendersons' of Bowling. They were contractors, delivering coal and everything. And there was horse-feed to deliver to coalmen all the way from Partick, through Whiteinch, away down and then back up through Duntocher, Drumchapel, and back. I'd load up the lorry on the Saturday, and at six o'clock on the Monday morning I'd be off. And it would be about six o'clock at night before I got home with the horse. One time I was down at Old Kilpatrick when the snow came, heavy snow. And I was there a week, delivering. I had to carry the stuff in a barrow.

THE BOMBING OF CLYDEBANK

During the war, we did the fire-watching. Every work did it. In Cleveden Lane, there was always one of the carters on duty, to cut the horses loose if there was a fire.

On the day after the Clydebank blitz, I had to take the horse out to Clydebank. They had sent the incendiary bombs first, set the place on fire. Then they followed up with the bombs. I had to go out with the grain – feedstuffs for the horses, cattle, goats, hens. And I led the horse through Clydebank. The place was still burning, still bodies lying. There was bodies hanging out the windows. Unspeakable it was. They set up a place where there used to be the shops, and they called it 'The Blizzard Store', where you could still buy things you needed. The Blitz Store, I suppose it was. I don't think there was a family in Clydebank that didn't lose someone. I led the horse through Clydebank and down to Demur and Bowling. The McFarlanes, where I used to deliver every week, they used to give me a cup of tea every time. One of the brothers had gone up on the roof to throw off an incendiary, and he was never seen again. Later on, I was delivering at a farm near Duntocher, and there was a shelter about 200 yards from the farm. The sirens went, and I put the horse into the stable. The family all went into the house, bar the son and myself. And this bomber came over, and dropped the bomb right beside the shelter. But the bomb fell in to the soft ground, and the earth went everywhere. And the farm windows all went in. The whole place shook, the whole farm. If it had hit solid ground I don't know what would have happened. When the bomb dropped we dived straight into the stable. But we were all right.

LIVING UNDER THE BOMBS

When we were staying in Highcraighall Road, they were always dropping bombs, trying to hit the power station there, what they called 'The Four Lums'. One time we just made it into the bomb shelter. The shrapnel was stotting off the railings as we ran, and as we got into the shelter it hit the shelter. Inside the shelter we did our best. I got the carriage-candles off the horses – thick candles, they were, about two inches thick, and we'd put them in an earthenware pot, with another earthenware pot on top. And it would amaze you the heat they gave off. And another one would play the mouth-organ, just to take away the atmosphere. My mother-in-law lived down by the Govan Road, and we moved over there. And near this house, we heard it, there was a whole building hit, right next to Stevens' Yard. And when we went to see it, everything was hanging out of it, furniture, people, everything.

We got word that my niece's man – my eldest sister's daughter's man – was taken prisoner by the Japs. He never came back. I remember when the soldiers came up to see her, to tell her what had happened. When he'd been taken to work on that railway, he had known what would happen. He'd asked them, if they ever got out of it, to go and see her and tell her. And he never came back. He'd used to busk at times with the accordion before the war.

Later on in the war, I was going out through Knightswood with the horse – just a young horse it was. And there was an accident. I was in hospital for weeks. I couldn't remember a thing about it. 'You're a lucky man, Bobby,' they told me. When I came round, my first thought was for the horse. 'Is the horse all right?' They wouldn't tell me. The horse was killed and the lorry was in bits – hit by a drunk driver. It wasn't his first offence, but he kept his job, with Tennents' Breweries. I'd a fractured skull, with a broken leg and a broken arm.

I thought, 'They've nae time now for horses.' And after that I went to work with the Highways Department.

THE PEACE

I'll never forget the end of the war. I was with the Highways by that time, and we were working in Hough Road beside the Kelvin Hall. We had all our barricades, planks, trestles, all our lamps and wooden lamp-posts, on barrows, all piled up. But when we came out the next morning ... nothing. They'd been celebrating the Victory. There wasn't a tool, not even a barrow. It was all burned. The bonfire had taken them all! We seen the ashes, that was all. Apparently some of the huts went, too. They came and told the watchmen just to go home: everything would be all right. And they burned the huts, the spades, brushes – there was nothing left. Bar the ashes and a hole in the road!

REMEMBERING TODAY

I was always connected to the Church, but I couldn't always go. Nell and I used to go to St Kenneth's in Linthouse, but we went even more to the Mission. But when I gave up the grain trade and went to the Highways I was often out at night with the lamps in the fog or with the ashes in the frost.

God doesn't make war. It's Governments that make war. The Lord provided fields. The big-money ones have taken them. God gives us water. Now they're taking that. And war is still going on today. Look at Ireland, with the bombing and the fighting and the innocent people dying. No. It's not God that makes war.

And today I think on the ones that died, and the ones that's alive still, in Army Homes. Quite a lot of ones I knew was lost. I think everyone's the same.

————— ««◆»» —————

Robert Softley Ross, Bobby, was born on 4th January 1913. His father worked as a carter with the railway, though soon after Bobby was born he had to go off to serve with the Army in the Great War. There were poor days. At the turn of the century, Mr Ross had been an Army blacksmith, shoeing Army horses in South Africa during the Boer War. When Bobby left school, his brother bought him a hand-barrow and Bobby sold brickets, or fruit, or fish. Then he and his brother got a horse and lorry, and at one time they had six horses, delivering all kinds of goods, mostly grain. Through an eye injury, Bobby was turned down for war service, but he worked with the local council's Highways Department for thirty-three years.

In winter he would be called out to salt the roads when nights became frosty. They had no phone in those days, so he just had to make his way to work if it turned cold. It was said that he put a wet mop out the window, and if it froze he'd go to work. And his wife, Nell, used to

pour boiling water on the mop to give him extra hours
of sleep.

Over the years, Bobby and Nell have sharpened their
wits on one another, to the amusement of their friends.
On their sixtieth Wedding Anniversary, they received a
telegram of congratulation from the Queen. They came
to the church on the Sunday, and at the entrance Bobby
was telling people how after these sixty years he would
do it all again. Hearing him, Nell said, 'Well, he'd have
to find someone else to dae it wi'!'

Helpful and unselfish to a fault, Bobby lived to be
ninety years of age.

1990

Mrs Robina Miller

- In South Africa, Nelson Mandela is freed from Robben Island after twenty-seven years in prison.
- The Iraqis' 'Super-gun', made by Sheffield Forge masters, is seized in Britain.
- Beirut hostage Brian Keenan is released after 1,597 days of confinement.
- Iraq invades Kuwait. Saddam Hussein negotiates peace with Iran.
- President Gorbachev is given new powers to reform the Soviet economy.
- Forty-five years after the end of the Second World War, East Germany and West Germany are re-united as Germany.
- The Tories oust Mrs Thatcher as Prime Minister, and replace her with John Major.

In 1990, Mrs Robina Miller is living now in one of a group of Pensioners houses. She is visited regularly by her son, and her grand-children, and she still likes to attend the Friendship club at the church each Wednesday afternoon.

CHILDHOOD, THE BOER WAR, HARD TIMES

I can mind the old days, before the trams, at Bridgeton Cross. I remember there used to be a coach stand at Orr Street facing the

Olympia; and it was drawn by two horses and two men. But where it went to I couldn't tell you. I was only a wee girl when I mind o' that. And I can mind o' the big fire at the paint works; I was just nearby at my school.

And I mind when Mrs Young's husband came back from fighting in the war in South Africa – Kruger's War, they called it. I can always remember the man with the khaki clothes, and a kilt on him, and a Glen Garry bunnet, a black bunnet. Whenever I saw the man coming I flew out of the house, and in to my mother's, crying, 'There's a man wi' a gun in Mrs Young's' – I stayed in 7 George Street, up off Orr Street from Bridgeton Cross, in the house I was born in. I was about five or six, I suppose, then. Is that ninety years ago?

Robina Kane Hollinger was my name. We came from Ireland, I believe. My father was born in Belfast, and two weeks old he was brought to Glasgow, and he was baptised here. They say Hollinger means we're from Holland, but I don't know. When I was young I worked in service. My father was crippled and worked mostly in the firewood place. He'd been left without his mother when he was young, and his legs were crippled, and he'd to use two sticks. He'd been at school at Weir Street, what you call Kerr Street now, up at Bridgeton Cross, and he and I'd the same teacher, Miss Gillies. But he was oftener off the school than at it, knocked about with not having a mother, so he hadn't much education. And it was something the same with my mother. I wasn't brought up with nae silver spoon in my mouth, I can assure you of that. Nae Parish, nae money. I came through hard, hard times, that people will never know. I'd go out and wash stairs, 3d [*1 pence*] a time for a big band of stairs.

I was just a day before sixteen when we had a wee bit of trouble in the family, and I had to go away off into service. In Arran, it was, Corrigill's Farm, at Brodick; Mr Kelso. It was terrible. I never got any money, bar one day I got a shilling on the day of the market, the first Saturday in June when they got together to sell the cattle, and had a day of carnival. All the months I was there I never got paid. And I missed the wee ones. And for all it was a farm we never knew what it was to get a pot of soup made. Do you know what we lived on? Rabbits from the hill, rabbits and potatoes. And it was always the breast bit I got, and you know how much meat is on that. And when they spoke, everything was Gaelic: I couldn't understand a word. So in the end I ran away. A visitor to the farm one day had been sorry for me, and gave me a half crown [*12 pence*]. And I used it for a fare on the boat. The Parish thought I must have swum back to Glasgow.

I got back to Glasgow. But I had trouble getting work in service because I was only 4 foot 11 inches tall; that was the bogey. I used to serve Lady Yarrow when she visited the lady I worked to, and she said I'd have worked for her in a minute if I'd been just a couple of inches taller. I used to have to look after my mother, too, because she took turns, and would just go down like a log. I'd go to look after her, and that's how I never went out much, or played much with other children like other lasses did.

MARRIAGE AND WAR

I was married when I was eighteen. Mr Lennox. And we lived at 700 Shettleston Road – it used to be 80 Main Street, but they gave it a new number. Mr Lennox was a miner, so he never had to go to the war. Like all the others that was doing other work he wore that band: what did they call it? – a Derby Band. He was a clipper-on of the hutches. When the hutches came down loaded with the coal he had to clip them on. He was in the Brochnie [*Barrachnie*] pit – pit's closed years ago – out the Baillieston way.

I never had much time to think about the war. I'd too much to think on: where we were going to get the next bite of meat fae! But you knew there was a war on, all right. You couldnae get sugar, you used to have to get candy balls to sweeten your tea with. If ever any sugar came, you had to take your chance and wait in the queue to get some, and away down to the market to stand and get a bite of butcher meat.

I remember the night the soldiers all marched away to the war from the HLI [Highland Light Infantry] Barracks at the corner of Main Street and Muslin Street. It was a Friday night, and the place was black with people. I didn't know very many of them. I was very quiet-natured. I used to play the mouth-organ – I'd pinch my father's mouth-organ and take it down to the work, and I'd play for the girls to dance. But I hadnae cla'es to go to the dancing with them, just very quiet I was.

We seldom had papers. My man was on the afternoon shift. My grandfather and him used to sit and discuss the war. My grandfather was one of the best cork-cutters in Glasgow – cutting the cork out for the bottles and jars, medicine bottles and the like. They said he was the smartest of the lot. He used to work in a wee place over from the High Court, right beside where there was an old tabernacle for the Jews.

People say there was telegrams when anybody got killed, but that's a lot of nonsense. People round us never got telegrams. It was the papers, *The Citizen*, *The Times*, and *The News* – they were only a ha'penny a time – see the price of them now! And if there was anybody killed they'd print their name there.

My man's brother was killed in the war, so he was. He had been in India for seven years, and was just home for a fortnight. And then he was away to the fighting line. And two months later he was shot. The Dardanelles it was, I think.

It seems he'd been sleeping and he was desperate for a cup of tea. He'd just written a letter to his mother and he'd put it in his breast pocket. So there was a wee cottage just across from where the trench was. And he went to get over to it. 'Charlie, Charlie,' his friend called, 'don't go up there. There's a sniper there!' 'But I must get a cup of tea,' said Charlie. And just as he said it the fellow went to pull him off the parapet. And the sniper's bullet went right through Charlie's heart, through the middle of the letter to his mother, and through the head of the pal that was pulling him down. A young fellow wrote all this to my sister-in-law: he had seen it all. She had it published. All they kind of things used to be in the *Weekly News*. And there was a photo of the letter with the hole right through it.

My man died in 1917. He was only twenty-four. He was the first victim of the Asian flu. A fellow had come to work with them in the pit, and he worked with my man, and the doctor said he must have been the carrier. Only a week's illness, and he died.

WIDOWHOOD AND WORK

About a week after my husband died, there I was with the three wee ones. Lottie was three, Hughie was two and Lizzie was just seven months. The minister from the Parish Church came down to see me and he asked what did I do before I was married. I told him I'd worked in the Bolt Work in Rutherglen, and in the mills and all. But I said the work I liked best was the Bolt Work – the heavy iron, heavy machinery, that's what I loved. He said, 'Would you take a wee job if you thought you could get it? You're a young woman.' (I was only twenty-two in the February.) So he spoke to a man in Beardmores and I was started work within a week. You got a week to learn with another person. And I was only a week working on my own on my machine when I was sent for. The Head Man told me I'd broke the record output. It was the big caps for the artillery shells. They came from the furnaces, and we had to take the rough off on a big, big turning lathe. It was in a wee mill I worked, just at the bridge at Camlachie, and the Head Man came up from Parkhead to see me. I loved working with iron, so I did.

Four days after my husband died, I got this wee text from the Sweetie works, Buchanans, I've always kept it. I found a frame for it at the Barras. From Psalms: 'He shall direct thy paths.' And ever since then the Almighty's guided me. He had directed my paths.

THE END OF THE WAR

The Armistice came in 1918. But I didnae know the war had finished. There was nae wireless, nae television. I think it was my brother coming in from his work that night that told us the war was over. And it was a good feeling to know that it was over.

But I remember shortly after the war we saw the big silver Zeppelin as it flew over. And it was about that time that Mr Wheatley went in as a councillor. He lived just round the corner from us in Shettleston. Him whose son was that Judge that died a few months ago – Lord Wheatley.

The end of the war didn't make nae difference to me, anyway. My life just had to go on the same way. I was a widow with three wee ones. But I remember going up to this woman's house – she'd been a neighbour years before – and I had wee Lizzie in the shawl. And I met this Mr Miller who had been brought up with them, and he'd lost his wife and he'd a grown family. And we got married in 1921 and I went to live in Rimsdale Street back in Bridgeton. And we had three more wee ones: George, but he died when he was one; Margaret, who died when she was ten; and William, and he was forty-one when he died.

THE MISSIONS

It was really the Mission halls that kept me going. I had nae cla'es for the church. The Missions suited the working class: you hadn't the wherewithal to buy the clothes for the church. The main one for me was in Bell Street. Mr Galloway was years and years there. And there was a wee Mission in Muslin Street. It was the nice singing, and the cheery tunes. And I loved to sing, 'There is a gate that stands ajar', 'A sinner was wandering at eventide.'

I got converted one time in Green Street Mission. On a Sunday I went to the Tent Hall at dinnertime. You got a big jug of soup in the winter, and a big jug of rice and milk in the summer. Up in the gallery were the better-off ones, and they got a wee china cup of tea; but downstairs it was a big jug for us!

And there was the open meetings at street corners. I sang at the street meetings. I had a good way with a tune, and a nice contralto voice.

And it was the Mission halls that kept me going. And I've always felt it was the Almighty who directed my path – that wee text from Psalms, I've always kept it. My mother taught me to say my prayers. And I say them every night yet. And two weeks ago, when I was feeling very ill, I tried to get somebody to come. But it was my neighbour, Lizzie, that I asked to come and help me with my prayers. Yes, I still say them every night. I never swore, and I never took drink. And if I wonder how I'm still able to remember things so clearly, I know it. The Almighty, it's His doing.

OTHER WARS

In the Second War my son, Hughie, went away overseas, and so did Lizzie's man. But they both came back safe. I worked in the Navy Stores in Fordneuk Street, and often we'd to put away the clothes that got returned from those that had been lost.

And now there's war in the air again. I've no head for politics. It's terrible for thousands to suffer over the head of one man. But I don't understand it. And I don't watch about it on the television. Whenever there's pictures of wars I put it off. I can't stand wars and I can't stand enmity.

ARMISTICE

And on Armistice Day I remember all my family. I'll think of the poor souls whose clothes came back in to the Navy Stores. I'll think of my brother-in-law, Charlie, killed in the Dardanelles. But there was too many for me to be able to think on them all.

And I think it'll take you till next Armistice Day to write all this down!

―――――――❖―――――――

Mrs Miller was born in George Street in Bridgeton, Glasgow. Given the name Robina Kane Hollinger, she was always known as 'Beeny'. In her young days, her family lived through hard times, and Beeny knew what it was to go without good clothes or enough to eat. She had great strength of character, and felt no bitterness about the burdens she had had to carry. She had weathered many sorrows: she was mother to six children, but when she died only her son Hugh was still alive to mourn her. To the end of her life her small, stocky figure was a familiar sight going about to the shops and to church meetings, and at home her strong capable hands did the housework and the cleaning until her death at the age of ninety-seven.

1991

Mr William Sweetin

- Operation 'Desert Storm' is the name given to the war campaign launched against Iraq to liberate Kuwait. The 100-hour land war crushes the forces of Saddam Hussein.
- Internal revolts grow in war-torn Iraq.
- Civil war looms in Yugoslavia, as Slovenia and Croatia declare independence.
- South Africa is re-admitted to international sport.
- President Gorbachev is toppled by a coup.
- Hostage John McCarthy is released from captivity in Beirut.
- Robert Maxwell drowns in the Atlantic, leaving financial chaos in his publishing empire.

In 1991, Bill Sweetin has been retired for five years, and he has established himself at home in charge of shopping and cooking. He and his wife, Margaret, have two children, both married and living in Aberdeen.

FAMILY LIFE AND THOUGHTS OF WAR

There was seven of us children in the family altogether, six boys and our sister. One of the brothers died when he was just young. At the time I was called up I was working beside my father in the flour mill, the Riverside Mills. I went in there at the time because they paid an extra three shillings a week, that's an extra fifteen pence a week, over and above what I was getting where I had been working, serving my time as a sheet metal worker with Thermotank. (I'd started off in Massey's as a message boy when I left school at fourteen. When I went for the job they said to me, 'Can you go a bike?' 'Yes,' I said. Two years later they produced a bike!)

My father had been a piper in the First War, a piper with the HLI [*Highland Light Infantry*]. He used to say, 'I'm one of the lucky ones.' He survived the war, you see. He used to talk about it, about the trenches and the mud. But we weren't that interested when we were wee. He had badges and medals from the war – and his pipes. And he had his chanter. He used to play the pipes quite a lot. Yes, in the house. You used to hear all the doors slamming when he started – the neighbours going away to the pictures – just the way they do when I get out my saxophone – 'There, he's at it again!'

My father taught the pipes to the boys in the Boys' Brigade in the church in Kinning Park at the corner of Cornwall Street. I tried the chanter but it was the saxophone I played, and then the clarinet. I got the sax for my fourteenth birthday. And I loved Benny Goodman, Artie Shaw, Tommy Dorsey. And I saved up for a clarinet. A friend of my mother's had a wee band and we played at places, nothing very big, just Church affairs, like Bible Class dances. And in the Kingston Halls, and at small weddings. We enjoyed it that much, it was a surprise when they gave you money!

We stayed in Tower Street, Scotland Street, and then moved out to Shieldhall Road. We came through the Church, Life Boys, Sunday School, Bible class. I never thought much about whether the war was right or wrong. But I just knew I didn't want to leave my family. I suppose I was a right 'fearty'. I think most men felt the same. Of course when I was in the army there were some of the real hard Glasgow men, who knew exactly what they would do to Gerry when they got him, but mostly we all felt the same, I think. And I've always been open that way – not afraid to say how I felt about it. My father was the same he told me. For it was even worse in his day, the slaughter. And all my brothers didn't need to go – they worked in the shipyards, and so they were to stay here. My brother Danny, a joiner, he went into the RAF later, and went off to Burma. But he always was one for the travelling, a go-getter. But my brothers didn't have to go. I should have been thinking it was a blessing they didn't have to go, but I was thinking instead 'Why me?' I just didn't want to go.

BASIC TRAINING IN THE BLACK WATCH

I was twenty when I was called up in June 1940. The call-up papers arrived and then it was a month before I left for the Black Watch base near Perth. There was no medical or anything. I think if your body was warm they took you. That was the infantry for you. The night before I left we had a party at home. My mother always seemed to have plenty of food – the teapot was never off the hob. I think we would have had steak pie and maybe, even in the wartime, she managed a dumpling – I always loved a dumpling. I went by train to Perth the next day. I didn't know anyone else who was going and I was really scared. A few of us got off the train and we all ended up in the camp at Scone Park. Those first three months we lived under canvas. I never was much of a one for the outdoor life, but I survived.

They really trained you: hard slogging, getting you disciplined, getting you fit. The villagers called you the 'whippets'. We learned rifle drill with the Lee Enfield, and there was the Bren Gun – no-one wanted to have to carry that: it was too heavy. At the end of the three months they picked a draft to go overseas. At the time I was very disappointed not to be going off on that draft. They turned out to be for Monty's lot, the Desert Rats, so what a long fight of it they had from 1940. But I wasn't on that draft, and I was really just as glad. Because I always tried hard to do everything right – I didn't want those punishment fatigues – I really had had to be dragged into the Army, and I didn't want to be there. I'd rather have been home.

TWO YEARS OF TRAINING

After that basic training we spent nearly two years mostly in England. We did do six months in Hawick, but we were six months guarding an airport in Andover down south. Then we went to Camberley, to a Guard's base. That was a right smart place, and nearly all day you were out in the square, marching, marching.

It was all training, training. I never felt fitter in all my life. We spent six months, too, in the Isle of Wight. That was a lovely place. But training all the time. We were training to fight. But we used to plot ways of getting out of it – we never wanted to fight. We used to talk of dressing up as nuns and hiding in the hills – like *Nuns on the Run*. But we kept up with the news all the time – that was our main topic, the war. And you made wonderful friends. I was just a Private all the time, and you got to know your own platoon very well. And when you were doing cook-house fatigues, I remember, you learned things about food you'd rather not know – nothing was wasted and you were that hungry you'd eat anything.

I spent my twenty-first birthday at Inveraray, doing invasion training in landing craft. And then, when we were down in Camberley, at the Guard's base, I was put on a sniper's course. Advanced shooting, at smaller targets, and moving targets, and much more practice. I'd always liked to try my hand at shooting: we'd had a dart gun at home and I'd always been good at it. I was certainly one of the best at that time, and so I got picked out for the sniper training.

I never had a lot of what you'd call pride in the regiment. See that bunnet, the Tam O'Shanter? I hated that bunnet. You'd catch sight of yourself walking past a shop window. At least it was the trews we wore and not the kilt. My legs were always thin. You hear them talk of a 'fine figure of a man', and I never really was one of those. More like a sparrow. And sometimes you'd get exhausted and frozen on those seven-day training stints. And sometimes you felt like greeting because you never felt war was right at any time, but you were in it anyway. And the Germans seemed like monsters, so you felt it was important to win the war. But I wrote home a lot – I got pretty homesick – I suppose I was a 'mammy's boy!' But I always used to go to Church Parades. With me being a churchgoer I did quite enjoy a service, singing the hymns. It was just part of me, and I wouldn't miss it.

OFF TO NORTH AFRICA

Then eventually the day came when we embarked for overseas. The Black Watch, the Royal Highland Regiment, we sailed out of Glasgow bound for North Africa. I always remember how you felt the heat when you landed at Algiers. When you were sailing into the port of Algiers, from a distance the buildings looked really white, shining in the sun. And you noticed how different the people were, the Arabs. We got off the ship, assembled at the quayside and we were marched off to camp. Getting ready for action meant we all got our heads shaved for the sand. We were all the same, all baldies. A lot of boiled eggs, we looked like.

The British Army was pushing the Germans back at the time under Field-Marshal Alexander. And the battlefront was just seventeen miles from Tunis.

THE TEN-SECOND WAR

We spent about three months on desert training and then we moved up towards the firing line. For three weeks we waited, hearing the noise of the guns in the distance. And then we were moved in closer and waited another week. Then they moved us right up to the battlefield. And after nightfall we moved up for the attack. You should hear the noise. Shells screaming and everything going: and the sky's all lit up with tracer bullets and different things. Little by little we moved forwards about half a mile – the whole Company, about 200 men. You crawled, you walked. They set off flares. You had to freeze. And now you were only a hundred yards from the German line. And you waited. You had your bayonets fixed – me being a coward, all I could think of was a big Gerry getting me on the end of his bayonet. Behind you were your officers, with their revolvers to shoot you if you turn and make a run for it – between the devil and the deep blue sea, you are, more or less. But I wasn't thinking about that. I was just thinking this was what we'd trained for and now it had to be done.

You'd been facing the line for about twenty minutes. Then, before you got the order to charge, the piper started to play.

That really got me. You'd come all that way to surprise them, and this piper comes. Maybe it's supposed to put the fear of death into the enemy – 'the Ladies from Hell', and all that, with the kilts. But you can't understand the brains that would give the order to the piper just as you were going to begin the charge and surprise them.

Then you're charging forward. It's sort of a suicide thing. The piper's playing and you're charging forward, the machine guns begin to fire. And I suppose that's what my father did, as a piper in the first war, piping the men into battle as they charged. And the machine guns were placed at angles, firing criss-cross as you ran, the bullets coming just above the ground. And suddenly it seemed as though there was a blinding flash in my brain. I think I kept going forward even after I'd been hit, trying to get beyond the line of the bullets. You'd rather get it in the heart, and finish off quick. I'd thought about all that through my training – especially when we were in North Africa near the firing line.

A machine-gun bullet had got me through the leg, near the ankle. I remember that it felt as though my big toe was trying to touch my heel, before I blacked out. Those years of training and my battle lasted ten seconds.

RECOVERY

When I did come to, it was later in the day. There were six of us lying on stretchers and I know that I heard at least two of them dying. And the next thing I knew we were in the field hospital, with the MO trying to attend to us. My leg was so badly fractured that I would never fight again. I would have to be discharged. As far as I know our Platoon lost quite a few that night. I saw only one of my friends. He had got it in the spine; he was paralysed from the waist down. He was the same age as me. He was from Kirkcaldy.

I was flown to an American hospital in Oran, and then I was put on a hospital ship after three weeks. We sailed past Gibraltar, I remember, on the way back to military hospital in Blackburn, Lancashire. I wrote to my parents that I was really all right, but I remember when my father came into the ward – he had come just to make sure I really was all right. It was a big surprise. I was so pleased to see him. And then my mother managed to get me brought up to the Southern General and I recovered my strength nearer home.

To me, war seems to be suicide. For the infantry anyway. But once I was home from hospital I could have kissed the German who shot my bullet.

REMEMBRANCE DAY

Remembrance Day is very important to me. I always notice as it comes nearer. I always have a poppy – though it's Margaret who buys it for me! That day – this day – I do remember. Especially during the silence. You see all the old soldiers in your mind. And I think of that friend who was wounded so badly, paralysed. And I'll think of other wars too. The Gulf War. I wished it hadn't been necessary – all the oil wells alight and the sea polluted with oil. And you can't help worrying for the boys, that there might have been a secret weapon, nuclear, or worse still, germ warfare. Yes, I do remember the ones that died. I think of them. But I like to be at home for the silence. It's too much being somewhere with others. Even today.

LIFE AND FAITH

And where is God in it all? I've always loved the Church and been a church goer from when I was young. But I sometimes think that if I had had a vision, something concrete, that would make me convinced, you'd feel everything was confirmed that you believe in. I'd want to see it, feel it, to confirm it.

But I am religious to a point: and you wonder if maybe God is helping you through. You look back and you wonder.

When I think of how lucky I've been. There's those that was killed. I survived. To be wounded, without being seriously wounded. To have gone to Springburn College, for the wounded, and learned the trade of mending clocks and watches. I enjoyed my work for years. My family life has meant everything to me – though my family won't know my serious thoughts about these things. And my saxophone. And my clarinet. And even though my ankle's swollen still, and I walk with a rolling step, I was even able to dance again.

You look back and you wonder.

———— «◉» ————

Bill Sweetin took a long time to recover from the wounds he received in the battle outside Tunis in North Africa. But he trained as a watch-repairer and spent the remainder of his working life at the trade. He was always ready to mend watches for friends. He lived with his mother and had seemed set in his bachelor ways. But in his mid-thirties, on a holiday in Belgium, he met Margaret Boyd. They married and in the course of time they had two children. Bill was musical like his father and he passed the gift on to his children. In his later years, he himself did not play publicly any more, but he played for his own pleasure and kept his saxophone under the bed. As they grew older Margaret suffered a stroke and Bill looked after her. He was in the city centre buying reeds for his clarinet just days before he died in 1996 at the age of seventy-six.

1992

Miss Jean Molloy

- British Prime Minister, John Major, and new Russian President, Boris Yeltsin, agree on nuclear weapons control.
- Maastricht, a small town in Holland, is the scene of the signing of crucial documents, which outline the process of growing European unity.
- Neil Kinnock resigns as Labour leader after the Tories win a fourth consecutive General Election.
- Serbian Death camps in Bosnia shock the world.
- Plans are announced to close thirty-one coal mines, and to make 30,000 miners redundant.
- Bill Clinton elected President of the United States of America.
- The Church of England votes to allow women to be ordained priests.
- The Nobel Prize for Peace goes to Rigoberta Menchu, an Indian woman in Guatemala.

**In 1992, Miss Jean Molloy is living in one of the pensioners'
houses. She's becoming a little deaf, but she still loves to
be in company, and she is in church each Sunday when
she's not away staying the weekend with her niece.**

———— ««◊»» ————

THE POOR DAYS

I was born in 1905, in the Gorbals; South Wellington Street. It's all changed now – they called it Lawmoor Street after that – and that's all gone now too, isn't it? I'd two brothers, James and Daniel, and two sisters, Charlotte and Nellie. I was the youngest, and they were all bigger than me. Not that I ever thought of myself as small, with high heels and all. When I was twelve I was bigger than all my pals. And I must have stopped at that point, I suppose.

My mother was left a widow – I was only four when my father died – he was just in his forties: enteric fever he died with. I mind when the men in white coats came and took him away on a stretcher after he died. That's all I remember of my father. And I was frightened they'd take me away too, I remember. I was only four. He was a chain-maker, the chain for the big boats. There was no union and my mother had to go and fight her case with P. W. McLellands. He was a good worker, too.

My mother had a hard life. It was real poverty. She was on the Parish and there was never much. Don't write this down. My brother Jimmy wouldn't go to school. So my mother used to have to take him herself. But she'd put him in the one gate, and he'd run straight out the other. So they put him to the Industrial School, out Riddrie way. And Jimmy learned swimming – he was a great swimmer – and he came out to be a baker. But sometimes he used to come home. And this time he told Danny, 'My, the Industrial's School's a great place. You get ham and eggs for your breakfast.' So did Danny not start plunking off school as well so as to get sent to the Industrial School and get ham and eggs for his breakfast. And so he did. He got sent to the Industrial School and he learned tailoring and played the cornet. But my mother could never give them ham and eggs – it was real poverty. Yes. Well, I suppose you could tell them that. For my mother was always cheery and everybody liked her. Her and I used to sit. She'd say, 'Come on and sing', and we'd sing.

She was Irish. Sarah was her name – my Dad's name was Daniel. 'From Londonderry on the banks of the Fail [*Foyle*],' she'd say. She was in Glasgow from her teens but she never lost her twang. She'd sit and learn me songs she'd been taught when she was young. We'd sing together as I sat combing her hair and sorting it for her. We were more pals than anything else.

You got a penny for your pocket money on a Saturday and that was it. A farthing of candy balls, dolly mixtures and the like, you'd get. With her Irish voice she called my brother Jimmy, and me Jinny. It was 'Jimmy' and 'Jinny' – and you'd never know which of you she wanted.

THE FIRST WORLD WAR

The two brothers were off at the war. The Great War, they called it. In the Navy. Jimmy went first: he was called up as soon as he was eighteen. We were all very poor: there was no special tea or anything, he just went away. Then two years later, when he was eighteen, Danny went off to the Navy too. They were both working as bakers at that time, one in Beatties, the other in the Co-operative Bakery in McNeil Street, just near where we'd moved to. Danny wasn't in the war that long. But my mother used to worry about them. She was always talking about them and watching the paper and listening to things. *The Evening Times* she got, looking at the lists of them that had been killed.

They used to write home. Asking for money! Well, no. Danny would send money home to my mother. And she'd send it off to Jimmy! I thought it wasn't fair, I mind of that!

I mind the Armistice when the war ended. I was thirteen. I was down in Darvel on holiday and I saw it in the paper, all the celebrations in London. When I got back home my brother was home on leave. He used to get me to wash his sailor's collar and his lanyard – and give me a penny. In peacetime he'd say 'I'll give you a penny for blacking my shoes.' And I'd do it, but I'm still waiting for the penny!

AFTER THE WAR, THE WORK

When I left school I went to the Co-operative Boot factory in McNeil Street. The Co-operative would send down to Hayfield School for the ones that was leaving and that was how I got started. It was men's boots and boy's boots. I fed the nails into this machine and the man worked the machine and it put the heels on the boots. And when the war ended,

I was told I would have to teach a boy my job because the men would be needing work now that the war was over. So I taught him my job and then I got my books. That's how it was in they days.

But I had a happy life. I don't mind my mother ever hitting me. We never fell out. I would always be helping her. We hadn't much furniture but I was always scrubbing it and polishing. And she would always tell people about me: she was quite proud of me and I was proud of her.

I was long enough without work. I tried all the works, the rag stores and everything but I couldn't get a job.

And I remember in the coal strike, my sister used to come up to see us. And she'd always some idea, something she'd heard. 'I hear there's coal out by Belvidere,' she said. So she and me went away out there with this pram to see what we could find. And she got a bag and I got a bag and we loadit them into the pram. And as we came along London Road the wheel kind of buckled and what a struggle we had to get it home. And we set the fire and we lit it. And here, did it not turn out to be tar. And as the fire caught the tar all started running out everywhere!

In time I got a job on the buses. I was fifteen years with Alexanders' buses, Alexanders' of Milngavie. I loved it on the buses. I remember one Sunday I walked it all the way from McNeil Street to Milngavie. That shift you took the people from Stepps to the chapel at Chryston. Three runs. Take them there; and then bring them back. And that was you finished: a good shift that was. It was a rare job, the buses, a cheery job. And my driver was a right comic. I did nothing but laugh with him from morning to night.

THE SECOND WORLD WAR

But then came the next war. And that niece of mine, Sadie, she lost her man in it. He was killed in Belgium, he was only in his twenties. And they had three of a family – she was to lose one of the wee ones, too. She never married again. She just doted on the children. Eddie. Eddie McGarrigle was his name. He was a good man. He worked in the railway. He never wanted to go to the army but he was called up and he had to go. My niece got evacuated. They never had much of a married life. She got word two years ago to go and see his grave. And that the first time she got to know how it happened, how he died. She went with her daughter, Charlotte. You do get sad. You think about them.

THE BUSES IN THE WARTIME, AND THE BLITZ

When you were on the buses at night time, during the war, it was very difficult. In the blackout, there was blinds on all the windows and you couldn't see out, and it was pitch black outside. Some passengers got angry when they missed their stop. One woman blamed me for not putting her off. I said, 'Can *you* see where you are? Because I can't.'

Coming into Glasgow, you could tell a wee bit where you were from the noises. There was the swish as you went under the overhead bridge after Anniesland. Then further in as you came to Byres Road you came to the parts where there was cobbles, a different noise. But it was all guesswork apart from that.

Two of the buses were turned into Ambulances. I mind when Clydebank was bombed they went away down to Clydebank. And as they were going down, the driver of the front bus was killed: a piece of shrapnel hit him in the neck. Just a young fellow he was, only twenty-one. Tommy. Tommy West, I think, was his name.

I remember one comical time when the sirens went. There was one neighbour, a great big woman she was. And her man was wee, and walked with two sticks. And they had five or more of a family. And this night the siren went, and we saw her running to the shelter with her pram. And she had her man in the pram, and the weans all running at the side. Comical it was, to see!

I remember one time in the blitz I was staying with my pal in West Street. We were just sitting at the fire as the sirens went. I said to my pal, 'Let's go out.' We went down the stairs, and we were standing in the hall. A landmine fell and I felt the windows come in, and glass go everywhere. And everything went dark. And the plaster fell from the ceiling on top of me. And I said, 'Cathy, where are you?' 'I'm here,' she said, 'I'm all right.'

We went up to the house the next day. The range had been blown right into the middle of the room. The windows were all in. Glass was embedded in the furniture. What would have happened to us if we'd stayed at the fire?

We were all right. But in the main road, the people, lots of Irish families, there was nothing left. Wiped out. We were sent up to the school. And people kept coming in: 'Is so-and-so here?' their mother, their families.

The morning after the Clydebank blitz, I was on this bus again. And when we got to Anniesland all the people who got on were from Clydebank. They were going out to stay somewhere in Bearsden. I couldn't take their fares. One was worse than another, crying. This yin had lost her mother, this yin her sister, this yin her house, everything. The inspectors must have known. For they stayed away that day, they never came on the bus. And I mind it, I couldn't take their fares.

And then when VE Day came at the end of the war, I was on the buses still. We came down the hill and there they were, dancing in the Square. Sailors, and soldiers, everybody was pals, everybody was dancing. My pal and I were in our uniforms I remember. We were all so glad it was over.

THE CHURCH AND FAITH

While I was on the buses I never went to Church much. You were up at 4.30 in the morning, and at night you'd to walk home from Buchanan Street. But I was very religious when I was young. I went to the Band of Hope, and I believed everything at the school. We did catechism, and saying prayers, and the hymns. I used to go to the Missions with my mother – it was women with shawls on them– a poorer class than the Church. My mother wore the shawl in they days. And the Minister at that place with the shawls, in Hospital Street, was a right comic. He suited the women just right.

When I was young, you didn't play outside on a Sunday if you were a Protestant. My friends were Catholics, and after twelve o'clock they could play. But I just used to walk with them.

I always liked the Bible stories and I do yet. Noah and the Ark, Lot and his wife, that pillar of salt. Adam and Eve. You know I'm still wondering about that. If God made Adam and Eve, just the two to start, how are there black people, and Red Indians? I still puzzle about it. I say, 'I'll have to ask Mr Miller about that.' And I like the story of the brides at the wedding with their lamps. And the story of the girl that lost her husband and stayed with her mother-in-law. It was nice, that, like real life. It was nice that, her staying with her mother-in-law. Wherever she went, she went with her.

I went back to Church before I came to Castlemilk. I went with my pal to the church in Waddell Street, Mr Wood's church. Then when I came here, I got friendly with Mrs Thurston, and she brought me here. And then I came with my friend Mrs Barrie, and my friend Susan, Susan Bell.

ARMISTICE DAY

I remember how on Armistice Day, whatever day of the week it was, the 11th, I remember how everything used to go quiet at eleven o'clock. And some of the lorries just used to go on, and people were quite angry about them. These are some of the things I remember and think about on Remembrance Day. I'm a person who doesn't worry about things. I've a cheery nature that way. But when you think about them you do get sad. Maybe the young ones will think about that today.

━━━━━ ‹‹◊›› ━━━━━

Jeannie Molloy was born on 23rd July 1905, and everyone called her Jean. She was the smallest of her family, not five feet tall. She was lovely to look at, and she enjoyed dancing. She had her romances, but never met the one she was to marry. After working on the buses she worked in a printer's, making Christmas cards. Then for more than twenty years she worked in the Glasgow Corporation printing works until she retired. She became very involved in the life of the local church and found most of her friends there. She was much-loved in the family, an aunt to many nieces and nephews. Each summer she went on holiday with her niece Sadie McGarrigle and her family. She spent each Christmas with them and was the life and soul of the party. She lived to be a great-great-great aunt, and the younger generations loved her as well, because her cheery nature drew them to her.

With assistance from Home Helps and family and friends, Jean lived independently until she was admitted to hospital just before her death at the age of ninety-four.

William Allison

George Godfrey

William Sweetin. His wife, Margaret, is on the left; Margaret's sister,
Dorothy, is on the right

Dolly Stevenson

Andrew McLelland

Richard McCracken and his wife Rose on their Diamond Wedding Day

Joan Victoria Knox

Christopher Drummond and his wife Sadie

*Cecilia McQuade (extreme left) and friends. Mary McLelland wife of
Andrew McLelland, is second from right*

Alfred Hamilton (front row, third from left)

Alfred Hamilton

Peggy Holding

Elizabeth Hunter

1993

Mr Andrew McLelland

- Two ten-year-old boys are charged with the murder of two-year-old toddler, James Bulger.
- An IRA bomb in the City of London causes damage estimated at £1 billion.
- United Nations forces attack Somali warlord General Aidid, but suffer a humiliating defeat.
- The United Kingdom ratifies the Maastricht Treaty.
- A peace accord, entitled 'The Oslo Agreement' is signed by Israeli and Palestinian leaders.
- F. W. de Clerk and Nelson Mandela share the Nobel Prize for Peace.
- John Major and Albert Reynolds, Prime Ministers of Britain and Ireland, sign a historic peace declaration, offering a peaceful path for Ireland.

In 1993, Mr Andrew McLelland, in his retirement, divides his time between the Pensioners' Action Centre where he is chairman of the management committee, and the local church where he acts as handyman, keeping the premises in good repair.

REMEMBRANCE DAY

When Remembrance Day comes, yes, you do remember. No. I don't say I dread Remembrance Day. But there's things I remember, people I remember. And I always wear a black tie on Armistice Day.

I remember how even after the war all the traffic stopped at eleven a.m. on the 11th November. And when I was on the buses I went every Remembrance Day in a black tie and white shirt, and with my medals.

FAMILY MEMORIES

My father had been in the Army for many years. The KOSB – King's Own Scottish Borderers. And it was from him I heard tales about the Army. That it was a good life. He was brought up in Coatbridge, and he was a miner before he joined up – and my first recollection was of my father working down the pit. We lived at Carnbroe. He told me of the Army days, of the Great War, World War One. How he'd fought in the Dardanelles; of his mates that never came back; the treacherous conditions they'd had to cope with; he said how British soldiers got on each other's nerves, and there was a lot of cruelty, as cruel as the other side. He told me about the mud at Passchendaele, three and four feet deep; sometimes trenches were so long you never knew when you'd come out.

But he told me you'd to be independent, to think for yourself, and I saw you could make a life for yourself. And to be honest, I didn't see a future for myself in Carnbroe. I thought if I stayed there I'd be down the pit.

By the time I was ages to go down the pit I'd moved to Glasgow to stay with an Aunt in Shettleston, though I didn't know anyone there. The city was like a new country to me. I was afraid of it, the size of it. There was only fifteen houses in the Miners Rows in Carnbroe! I'd heard a lot about Glasgow, and I was scared of it. But my first job was there; the Burroo School got me it – message boy in a grocer's in Kidston Street in the South Side. I was fourteen-and-a-half, a message boy with a bike.

But I knew I'd like the independence of the Army, makes you a man, teaches you all sorts of things. That's what I wanted. So I decided to enlist in 1938. War was already on the horizon then. But in those days civilians didn't like soldiers: thought of them as just crooks and vagabonds. Until after the war started. They'd to accept them then.

JOINING UP

My father had been in the KOSB and he was angry when I joined the Argylls. The first time I went to join up I wasn't eighteen, and my father refused to sign the Certificate. He said it wasn't the life for me. But I enlisted in Queen Street – me and a lad named Holmes.

A FRIEND

I'd never met him before, but we joined up at the same time. Holmes' Army number was 2982349. I've never forgotten it. The next one, 2982350, was me. We always knew each other's numbers. I was in 'A' Company, he was in 'C' Company. But we became good friends. He was heavier built than me, but the same age as me, and we got on really well.

A funny thing happened on that day, our first day at Stirling Castle. We met this fellow. It was *his* first day in the Argylls, too. A funny thing. But Holmes and me, we were the best of friends. During our training at Stirling Castle we'd been at each other's homes. He was quite shy, reserved. Just like I was then. William Holmes was such a good friend. Just what I needed. Now I'd say he was a Godsend to me: sent from above, such a good friend. But in those days God was far from my mind.

When our training was finished, we sailed from Southampton to Palestine: we were there when the war started.

EXPERIENCES OF WAR

There, in Palestine, we were trying to keep up the peace between the Jews and the Arabs. We used to have to be up in the hills, with our machine-guns, watching the Arabs moving ammunition from one place to another. I learned a wee bit of Arabic off the laundry man and woman who did our laundry. I remember the first time I came to Anderston, my father took me to the pub, and started boasting about me, and asked me to tell the time in Arabic. And I remember that he was very proud. 'My sojer son.' 'My boy.' He showed me off to everyone.

In Palestine, though I'd heard of Jerusalem and Jericho, there was only one time it struck me. A Padre took thirty of us to Jerusalem; he explained it all. Then, much later, when I started getting a wee bit of faith, and then started going to Church, they began to fall into place, those things he'd taught us about Jerusalem.

After the war started, we were moved to the Western Desert. It was in Sidi Birani that we saw the first action. Holmes was killed that day. The 10th of December 1940. We were in battle together. We had gone up the line against the Italians. It was the first attack we had made. We were advancing on foot. We were bombed that morning. We'd been beside a big Army tank. You talked away to yourself. You'd no idea what it would be like. Then we advanced.

I just saw him going down. You have no time to stop. You have to carry on. Two years we'd been together, training, up in each other's houses, photos taken together. It was my worst experience of the Army when he was killed. I was stunned. It was then I began asking 'Why?' Not, 'Why was he killed?' But, 'Why this war?'

Not long after Holmes got killed, I was blown off my feet, and I was wounded in the hand with a piece of shrapnel. They flew me to the coast in a bi-plane, to a hospital ship; and I sailed home. Holmes came from Springburn, and I went to see his parents. In a few months I was better, and they didn't take long to send me out again.

In 1942, I was in the tent this day. Sgt Maguire and Sgt Foy – he was from India, and then I knew him when he lived in Tormusk Drive – picked out thirteen of us. 'You're the volunteers,' they said. They took us for Ack Ack training for the Navy. At that time the Royal Navy couldn't protect all the merchant shipping, so we were volunteered for convoy duty. My first ship was called *The Nathie*, and it had only a small crew.

This day we got attacked, and we were watching for torpedoes. We avoided one. But a plane dropped another one and it hit. The ship keeled right over. The crew went for the lifeboats. But we didn't know what way to go. I jumped into the sea to get away. I started moving as best as I could. I wasn't a great swimmer. A man beside me in the water said, 'We'll do the best we can.' Then the German planes came and machine-gunned us. You're swimming, trying to save your life, and there are people you have never done harm to trying to shoot you. The sea was full of people, people swimming, people in boats. You could see the minesweepers that had been with the convoy; but they were frightened to come too close. The person beside me, I found out, was a Catholic Priest. We must have been in the water a long, long time. But we did get picked up by a small gun-boat. Until that day I'd had a closed mind about Catholics. But the encouragement I got from that man, that day, it changed my mind about a lot of things.

And then it was straight back to the convoy duty. The ship I was on next went to Libya, and then back to Malta. And I was there when the heavy, heavy bombardment of Malta came. That was simply terrible. Day in, day out, constantly. It's hard to describe. They were telling you to get shelter. But there was a small group of us; and no-one could tell us anything. We were walking about. We went about as if nothing could touch us.

When I was up the line, I was as good a soldier as any of them and that's not boasting. I was promoted Lance-Corporal up the line – and they say that's the place to be promoted. But of course, when things were quiet, and I went for a bite to eat and had a drink, I helped myself at the Officers' place; and they took the stripe off me. And I never used to think about God: if something went wrong I used to think it was some officer had put me in it.

SURVIVING

There was another time, in France, later on in the war, when I had to think about things. One day we were in a truck, eight or ten of us. It was camouflaged with canvas. The driver went too close to the edge of the ravine. The truck went over the edge and fell down the side of the ravine. After it had stopped turning over and over, the two lads each side of me was dead – broke their necks. And I was all right. On each side of me the lads died. This made me wonder, 'Why?'

And the ones who survived that truck, we went up on to the road, picked up another truck, and off to face the Germans. We got to this place, and they wanted five of us to go up to a canal. They just shouted out five names. And I was one. We were to find out if there was any Germans there. We'd an idea there was, but no-one had seen them. I was carrying the Bren gun; we got to the canal and lay down. At first we saw no-one. Then we saw a German truck on the other side. They dispersed. They must have spotted us. Next thing I knew I'd been wounded in the buttock. Shot right through the buttock as I lay there. And now there's bombing. They're bombing us, and we're bombing them. And I began to think, 'Is there anybody, anything, up there?' Instead of just saying the words, 'God help me', I began to start saying it more seriously. I don't know if you can understand me.

Anyway, I crawled back from the canal the best way I could, though it was very painful. I came home by plane. I had to lie on my stomach in the plane, and then even in the Hospital, Buchanan Castle. It took a wee while to get me better. But then I was back: sent out to France again.

And then again, one time we were in a battle, having a terrible, terrible time of it, bombs flying all over the place. We dug wee trenches. This bomb or whatever exploded and this piece of shrapnel struck my boot. I almost collapsed even before I looked at it. I remember this three or four fellows running over to me, and they took me to a First Aid post. I was transferred home once again. And I had to have two or three operations on my foot.

These are just one or two of the things that happened, that have made me think through the years.

THE GROWTH OF FAITH

My faith as it grew was very secret. If anyone had asked me what I was, then I'd maybe go to a Protestant Church Parade. But as for anyone thinking I'd be attached to a Church, nobody would know – I never showed it. I would never have criticised the Church. I'd a wee suspicion about people, but not about the Church.

I used to go to a Sunday school when I was in Carnbroe. My father was a well educated man, people used to come to him to get him to write letters for them. And he used to try to pump Christianity into us. We were taught right from wrong, to respect people and their families. And when I moved to Glasgow I joined the Salvation Army – but I should admit that that was for the sake of a trumpet!

But my father used to go to a Mission in Castle Street, and he'd carry a banner, and he'd preach at the street corner. But it never affected me. But I did copy a verse off him: John 3:16: *'For God so loved the world, that he gave his only begotten son, that whosoever believeth in Him should not perish, but have everlasting life ...'*

And I felt that there must be some God looking after me. I was too foolish, too careless, to look after myself. And I never felt any hatred for the Germans in the field.

HOW DOES FAITH ARISE?

I got a bit of faith in two other places. I've never been a person who thought myself a great guy. But when they two got killed in the truck, one came from the South Side of Glasgow. I went to see his mother. I got her address and went to Lawmoor Street to tell her how her son had died.

'Do you mind coming to St Francis's with me,' she said, 'to say a prayer?' I knew there was no way I could say 'No'.

And then, the person who couldn't do a thing for himself went to see Holmes's parents. This man had no courage in himself to do this. It didn't come from me, I tell you. That also helped me towards faith. That I, a man feart to face things, could do that.

For Remembrance Sunday, then. There you are. There's some of my thoughts, and some of the people I'll remember. I don't know if that's any good to you. But it's the best I can do.

Andy was one of seventeen children of a coal miner and his wife, and he grew up in the miners' rows in a small

Lanarkshire mining village. He was a regular soldier for many years, and after returning to civilian life he worked at a wide variety of jobs. But at that stage of his life he was an unhappy man, difficult to get on with. He drove buses with the Glasgow Corporation, where he was, by all accounts, a law unto himself when it came to whether or not to stop to pick up passengers. Life did not go smoothly for him, and for many years he took no care of himself or his wife and family. But he turned his life around. He won a place of respect once more in his family and in the local community. As an Elder in the church he was consulted for advice by a wide range of people. He was the Chair of the management committee of the local Pensioners' Action Centre.

Andy and his wife Mary are very highly regarded in the area. They are grandparents and great-grandparents, and in 1995 a huge family party honoured their Golden Wedding Anniversary. In 1997, in the New Year's Honours list, Andrew McLelland was awarded an MBE for services to the community. Mary now looks after Andy, and he needs a Zimmer to get about. But he has an electric buggy, and can drive on the pavement to the Pensioners' Action Centre for his lunch and a chat with friends. While Andy is out Mary goes visiting people in the hospitals and homes round about.

1994

Mrs Dolly Stevenson

- Mortar bombs fired into Sarajevo market-place kill sixty-eight people as Serbs attack the city.
- Bullets fly in the streets of Johannesburg, South Africa, as the date of the first all-race elections approaches.
- Rwanda horror reveals deaths of one million people in ethnic civil disorder.
- Nelson Mandela is sworn in as President of South Africa.
- The Channel Tunnel is opened.
- John Smith, the Labour Party leader, dies. Tony Blair is elected as the new leader.
- Roll-on Roll-off ferry *Estonia* sinks in the Baltic Sea, with the loss of 912 lives.
- IRA and Loyalist paramilitaries in Northern Ireland announce a cease-fire.
- Russian troops storm into Chechnya.

In 1994, Mrs Dolly Stevenson, now widowed, lives in a quiet street of pensioners' houses. She has brought her family up in Castlemilk. Her daughter, Ray, a doctor's receptionist, lives not far away and Dolly enjoys visits from the family.

BORN INTO A TIME OF WAR

All my life I've been involved in the war. My father and my uncles, my brothers and me; and one of my sons was on alert in 1958, in the Suez crisis.

I was born in 1915, in the second year of the Great War. My father never saw me when I was born; he was away in France with the Seaforth Highlanders. Then he was wounded, shrapnel in the leg. He was two months in hospital in the South of England and then straight back to France because they were running short of men. So he never saw me even then.

Then he was at the Battle of Mons, and he took a bullet through his right lung, in at the front and out of the back, and he was left for dead on the battlefield. My mother heard he was missing, presumed killed. She was a widow, as she thought, for two years. Then she had news from this hospital in Wales. It seems that, after the battle, two Red Cross men at Mons had seen a slight movement in him, and took him to the dressing station. And they sent him to this hospital in Wales. He was in a terminal ward. He didn't know anything, couldn't speak. The doctors had given up. But this American nursing sister tried a new treatment on him to stop haemorrhaging, and she managed to get him to tell her his name and where he came from. And soon he was well enough to come home.

I remember sitting on this strange man's knee, he had a kilt on. He was my Dad, they told me. But I'd a great job understanding. I was three at the time.

My father's two brothers were in the war as well. One was wounded in the hand. He was a piper, piping the troops over the top at the Somme. Andrew. He was shot through the hand and could never play the pipes again.

The other brother was in the Cavalry. My father was in a trench. The cavalry were retreating and jumped back over this very trench. The two brothers hadn't seen each other for two years and they met there like that. Later my uncle's horse was shot under him, but he survived. He brought the horse's tail home as a memento along with a German helmet.

My grandmother's three sons all came home from the war. But in her wee row of cottages there was a woman whose three sons were all lost.

FAMILY LIFE

My father came from a farm in Swordale in Ross-shire. Alexander McKay. My Grandfather was dying – he had been gored by a bull, and nothing could be done – and he asked my mother to give his name to her unborn child. But the baby turned out a girl: me. So that's me; Donaldina Georgina McKay! (Though I was Dinah for long enough, and then Dolly.)

We lived in Tarlogie Estate, near Tain in Ross-shire, which belonged to Count De Serra Largo. He was a Scot, a McKenzie, who had been a naval Captain, and had been awarded the title by Spain. I remember his funeral, with his naval uniform on his coffin.

My father was game-keeper on the estate. The Count was my Godfather – he carried me into the Church at my baptism, my father being away at the war. When my father came back from the war he went back to his work – his job was still there for him. And he lived until he was seventy-one.

On the cold winter nights, when we were snowed in, he would tell us stories of the war, some so terrible you could hardly believe them. He told us of the young German boys, only sixteen years of age, dying in the battlefield, crying for their mothers. He didn't like having to go against them. And as I grew up I was never without thought of how he had suffered, and what effect war had on everyone. I always believed in God. As a little girl I'd sing hymns. We were brought up that way, and I always trusted in God. We went to church every Sunday. If we couldn't get to church in the winter we would have a service at home in the lodge – the house we lived in at the entrance gates of the estate.

When I left school, I was a Lady's maid to the Countess. There was nine of a staff in the house: housemaids, cook, and butler. I was upstairs all the time, attending to the Countess, with a bedroom along from hers. The others were all downstairs. I used to go to church with her, then; we sat in her private box, the Tarlogie Gallery, with her crest on the front of it. After the Count died, the estate was sold to the Forestry Commission, and my father had to move. He became game-keeper on Carbeth Estate at Killearn: we all moved south to Killearn.

MY OWN GENERATION AT WAR

I trained as a nurse at Stirling. War was impending, and Killearn Hospital was being built. I married George Stevenson in 1936. He was a painter from Glasgow, painting the new hospital. And being a painter, he worked throughout the war, camouflaging aerodromes and battleships. He was all over the country, never at home for long.

I joined the Red Cross, to go over to France to help the troops. But my father did not approve of it. He said war was too terrible for a woman to go to the battlefields. So I stayed nursing at Killearn. Of my three brothers, the oldest went to the Navy, my youngest two were called up to the Army. My father advised them too: he said, 'Don't go looking for medals or glory.'

My second brother was taken prisoner at St Valery, and he was a prisoner of war for five years. For two years we did not know if he was alive or dead – just as it had been with my father. He was two years in hospital with a sniper's bullet wound in his head. My youngest brother was evacuated from Dunkirk. My oldest brother was involved there, serving on HMS *McKay*: every soldier he pulled out of the water he looked to see if it was his brother. I remember when he came home he sobbed his heart out on my father's bed.

Later he was serving in the English Channel. He was a smoker, and he was having a break on deck. A torpedo split the boat in two and he was one of the only eleven who survived. The ship went down in seconds; there were 500 or more on board. Then he served on a minesweeper, and his ship was blown up. Seriously injured, he was transferred to Killearn Hospital, and I nursed him there myself.

NURSING AT KILLEARN

The wounded started to come to Killearn from the first months of the war. The war injuries were terrible; people with arms off, legs off, head wounds, chest wounds, everything. I saw more gore in a week than a nurse today sees in a lifetime. Our own boys were the first to arrive. Later on Germans, Italians and Poles. Wounded prisoners came, and were lying in the same wards as wounded Scots and English boys. There would be a bit of narking. As soon as the Germans were better, they went to the prisoner-of-war Camps; our own boys went back to their regiments. The prisoners were put to work in the fields. I remember one young man cut his hand, all down to the wrist. I wrapped a towel round it. One guard came with him and me, walking up the village street to the hospital. Some of the old men and women gave me a bawling out, 'Never mind the German so-and-so! Let him bleed to death.' 'And your own brother's a prisoner of war!' I told them it was my job. And he was human like them. I was disgusted. He showed me a photo of his wife and family, and he didn't know if they were dead or alive. When we brought him back after he'd been seen to, my Dad made me strong tea for him and looked after him. My father didn't hate the Germans because of those young boys he saw at the end of the war. 'It was a case of shoot or be shot', he used to say, and he didn't hold a grudge.

In the hospital the young German soldiers would cry out at night for their 'Mutti', their mother. And they'd call 'Gott im Himmel'. 'God in Heaven!'. We had to help them. Some of them were very courteous, very polite, 'Danke schoen, Danke schoen.' The post mistress married a prisoner of war. And people wouldn't speak to her. We had another episode. Rudolf Hess was kept in the hospital, in a little Ward by himself for two nights. I saw him leaving, as close as I am to you. We knew who he was.

CIVILIAN CASUALTIES: CLYDEBANK

Early in the war, they brought children from the Sick Children's Hospital – the ones who couldn't go to the shelters. About forty of them came to Killearn. One night I was on duty as the planes came over. The hospital had a big red cross on the roof, but bombs were often dropped all round us, off-loading the last bombs before flying home. This night, the Anti-Aircraft guns opened up, and shrapnel was falling on the roof. The children were terrified.

When Clydebank was bombed, I went in one of the ambulances to collect the injured – making them comfortable, stopping the bleeding. There would be four to an ambulance, travelling at crawling pace, without lights. We would collect them at dressing stations where some had First Aid. We saw more dead than living after the bombing. Little bundles and big bundles. It was a nightmare. We collected the injured in Maryhill as well. We picked up one woman who had a lot of glass in her back. We had to lie her on her stomach all the way to Killearn. And we had to do what we could for her. We had no time to think, no time to be squeamish. I can see it all in my mind's eye. I used to dream about it.

For three nights in a row, Clydebank was bombed that time, and three nights I was out with the ambulance. I remember sitting at the table in the canteen in the morning, and I fell asleep across the table. I've often thought what we could have done if they'd had helicopters for the wounded then, like they have now. I was always keen on amateur dramatics and I remember one night, in the wartime, we were singing our last song on stage. The planes started coming over, and instead of our proper song we sang 'Land of Hope and Glory'. And some wounded soldiers came up on to the platform to sing it with us.

THINKING BACK, THINKING FORWARD

I kept on nursing, even after George, my first born. We moved to Glasgow, to Bardowie Street in Possilpark, in 1945. I often thought of my brothers, hoping they would come through all right. Then when the war in Europe was already won they used this horrific bomb in Japan. We had no inkling that they'd been making this bomb. We saw some of the damage in the picture house.

I spoke to nurses who had been prisoners in Japan. They said they'd never seen anything so awful as what the women and children suffered from the bomb. One I met was a sister in Robroyston. She was just young. But her hair was pure white. Three of them had been captured along with the soldiers. They suffered, all the soldiers suffered, and more besides. She went down to less than four stone in weight. She *hated* to see any food wasted in the Hospital. She looked like an old, old woman.

During the war we never complained. But, when it was over, I wondered what was gained. All these people shot, maimed. We had nothing left but dead men, dead women, children; sorrow; broken hearts; mothers losing their sons, wives losing their husbands. Like a nightmare you'd wakened out of.

Highlanders, though, always had to fight for what they wanted. You'll hardly ever hear a Highland soldier complaining about the war. They take it for granted that they are fighting men. Its just heritage they've got. My father, for instance. And he did believe in God. And we had to say our prayers every night. (I was too young to remember it, but there was a family story about my brother Charlie. When he was five he was saying his prayers: 'God bless Mummy and God bless Dad,' and so on. And he added, 'And God bless the German that shot my Dad.')

I did always trust in God. Being a nurse, I saw the suffering of both sides. I didn't want to doubt God. I used to say, 'Why is God letting all these things happen? We must have displeased Him.' And I used to think war was the work of the Devil. And I called Hitler the Devil. All the more when we saw the films of the Jews in those camps. Those poor, poor people, with their numbers printed on their arms. They were brought to Killearn too.

REMEMBRANCE DAY

Remembrance Day was always a special day in Tain. The Service wasn't in the church, but at the War Memorial in the centre of the town. A pipe band played laments; they'd march down the street. And a bugle would play *The Last Post*. The old soldiers wore their medals.

If the 11th of November was a school day, we had the two-minute Silence at eleven a.m. At our desks, standing for the silence. We took it very seriously. I remember one boy burst out crying in the silence. He'd lost his Dad in the war. And his Mum had died. And he was in the poor-house. There was a lot of orphans then. Now it's a Children's Home, then it was a poor-house.

I don't dread Remembrance Sunday. I feel all my family is round about me, my brothers and my Dad. I think they should be remembered, and not forgotten. I learned about the First War from my parents. My family learned about the Second War from us. I suppose today's young ones have to learn from us, too. I don't know whether they should be told the horrors of war – there are some things too terrible to speak of here today. But maybe they should.

For if war were to break out again, another war, the world would end. I often think, 'There will be wars and rumours of wars ...' as the Bible says. And I think it's coming true.

———— «◆» ————

Dolly Stevenson lived most of her adult life in Glasgow. She developed a Glasgow accent, but when she met with people from the Highlands she resumed her Highland voice. But some things are too difficult to say in any language. In the above account of her wartime experiences, she could not bring herself to tell an early event. In 1936, when she was twenty she married Ralph Mahon, an Irishman who was in the RAF. Tragically, when their son Alec was only two, Ralph was lost in the war. Alec was brought up by Dolly's parents.

In due course Dolly met and married George Stevenson; and, in Glasgow, they brought up their family of five. When George was forty-two he suffered a severe heart-attack, and there were difficult days for Dolly and the family. However, he worked on until he was sixty-three and died in 1982 aged sixty-seven. Although she lived so far from the countryside which she had loved as she grew up, Dolly enjoyed her Glasgow life, and she had a close friend in neighbour Mrs Peggy Holding. Dolly was at the head of a large family as grandmother to nineteen and great-grandmother to twenty-two of the youngest generation of all. She died at the age of eighty-three, a few days after going into hospital following a fall.

1995

Mr Richard McCracken

- The Talibans, 'the Students of Islam', prepare to capture Kabul, the capital of Afghanistan.
- Nick Leeson, futures trader, bankrupts Barings Bank, the exclusive bank used by the Royal family.
- The Federal building in Oklahoma City is bombed by Timothy McVeigh, a former US soldier, with more than 100 dead.
- Mel Gibson's *Braveheart* wins Academy Award for Best Picture.
- Pope John Paul II reaffirms the Roman Catholic Church's opposition to abortion, contraception, IVF treatment and euthanasia.
- A jury acquits former US Football and film star O. J. Simpson of the murder of his wife, Nicole Brown Simpson, and her friend Ronald Goldman.
- Bosnian Muslims open an offensive to lift the thirty-eight-month siege of Sarajevo.

In 1995, Richard McCracken is a tall, dashing-looking eighty-five-year-old, with a neat white moustache. He is very much a family man, enjoying his home life with his wife, Rose, and their daughter, Rita. He's as much a Glasgow Rangers supporter now as he was as a boy.

GROWING UP AMONG MEMORIES OF WAR

I was born in August 1910. My oldest brother, Joseph, went off into the First World War in 1914, and I don't ever remember seeing him until I was nine. I remember, I was round the back, and my mother shouted, 'There's someone to see you!' And I went in and he was there, still with his kilt on. When I was born he was seventeen, and he joined up at the start of the war. He was in Mesopotamia for four years and seven months, with no leave, none. He was in the Seaforth Highlanders.

My other brother joined up in 1916. That was Willie; Willie was in France. I remember him coming home, too. Joe was wounded twice; and Willie once. When Joe got married he stayed quite a distance away, but Willie stayed nearby. He took to drink, and he put it down to the way they poured it into them when they sent them 'over the top', as they called it, in the war. He was in the Royal Scots. He married Jeannie Sharp.

There was ten of us in the family altogether: Joe, Willie, Alec, George and me Richard; and the girls, Euphemia, Alice, and Alice – there was two called Alice, for the first wee Alice died – Jessica, and Teresa. We stayed then in Baltic Street. I was born in Preston Street, but that's Dunn Street now.

WORKING LIFE AND WAR

When war broke out that Sunday morning, Chamberlain was it? came over the wireless. I got called up. But my boss kept me out at first. I was working in the Dye-works, William McConnell, Dalmarnock Dye-works. It was in Davidson Street, just off Dalmarnock Road. I went in at fourteen, in the December. I'd have gone in straight from school, but I'd hurt my hand – I fell on the spikes when I was playing, and had to go to the Royal for six weeks. So my father took me to get a job at the cotton mill, where my sister worked, because I'd missed the chance of getting in beside my father at the Dye-works. The chance came again in the December, and so in I went. I went in at fourteen and came out at sixty-five: fifty years and eight months I worked there, with four years and seven months in the RAF in the middle. When I was forty I became a foreman. I was Violet McComish's gaffer then! [*Violet McComish has been a member of Castlemilk East Parish Church for twenty-five years.*] When I started in the cotton mill, I got 10/2 [*51 pence*] a week. I got nineteen shillings [*90 pence*] when I moved to the Dye-works; and by the time I was twenty-one I was earning £2.7.6 [*£2.35*].

When the war started we were dying khaki for the Army, the thread before it was woven into shirts. It came in hanks, and then the weft went through the dye, 188 threads over a drum, and up and over a paddle and it was wound on to bobbins. Then it went over to the drying section on a barrow. Then it would be off to Holland's Mill, or to Andersons or whatever – only the two mills then, though there used to be twelve in Bridgeton – to be woven into cloth for the uniform shirts, poplin shirts.

The big cheeses used to come to the work to check it for colour and so on. All in their uniform. So it was war work, right enough.

But a great mob of us had got called through to Edinburgh, and they'd asked you what you would like to do. I said I fancied the RAF. I suppose I liked the thought of being a pilot. But by the time I was called up I was thirty, and that was too old for that. I suppose I was a bit romantic about war at that time. When the bomb dropped on Allan Street, that was just before I got called up. 'When I get called up,' I said, 'Gerry won't be over again.' The RAF sent word. They gave me eighteen days. We were in our room and kitchen when the word came. We'd started out in the single-end in 35 Poplin Street, then we moved across the road to number 30.

First we were sent to Blackpool to get kitted out and jagged. Then we went to Morecombe for six weeks. There was 138 of us. They were mostly young lads, and I was thirty. But there was one guy forty-three or forty-four, and I used to do his guard duty for him at night. Then we were posted.

THE YEARS IN THE RAF

I was posted up to East Fortune, a wee airfield near North Berwick. We built that place. It used to be a TB Hospital, and they put the patients out and brought us in; 60 OTU, Operational Training Unit. We worked twenty-four hours on and twenty-four hours off. Pilots were training there twenty-four hours a day, night time and all. They had to practice take-off and landing. At night time we had to set out the landing lights, the glim lights, they were called. We'd go out with a wagon and set them along the runway, heavy they were, with a battery. The light was sort of hooded. You couldn't see them from above, but as the planes were coming in they could see the lights. I was there for two years, and by the time we left we had dug up the edges of the runway and put in cabling, and it was electric lights all worked with a single button.

Being posted to Scotland like that meant that I was one of the lucky kind, because I was always able to get home. Whenever the door opened I'd be off in a shot, back home to see Rose and the family. I remember a chap, Forsyth. After he'd done his six weeks in Morecombe he was sent to Alexandria. And his wife always used to say to Rose, 'How can your man always get hame, and ma man can't get hame?' And then he was killed on the shores of Sicily.

We were under fire, though, at East Fortune, I remember. Gerry used to come in and bomb the airfield at Drem, and one night we had one of our aircraft at the end of the runway with its lights on, and we had to run to turn them off. There were accidents, too. One man walked into a propeller. And another time, when they were doing 'circuits and bumps' – the pilot would wear black glass goggles, to make it like it was night time; and they'd circle the airfield and bump down on the runway – and this time after he'd bumped down he went to climb back up for another circuit when the plane just exploded in mid-air as we watched. And I'd joined up in May, and I got home at Christmas. When I went back to East Fortune we'd lost twenty odd aircraft, and six or eight pilots we'd lost. You were home for a day; come back and someone you knew was gone. I was always someone who made light of things, even if it was very serious. But you could never get used to it.

RAF INSTRUMENT REPAIRER

Then I was posted to Melksham, near Devises. It was in Wiltshire, and I did a sixteen-week course to become an instrument repairer. I'd done well in a test, and they said, 'Off you go on that course.' I wasn't one for volunteering. Then I was posted back up to Montrose, and I worked with a fully-fledged repairer. I used to replace faulty instruments. They called it a 'blind-flying' panel and it had six instruments. Look at the things they have nowadays. But then it was six: Rev. Counter, Rate of Climb, Altimeter, Airspeed. I'd fit a new instrument, and then we'd go up and test it. The Officer in Charge there was a footballer – he played inside-right for Fulham and for England. We were quite proud of him. Next, I was posted down to Sealand, at the Welsh border. That was a huge place: there must have been 1,300 of us, and I worked at a bench repairing the instruments, from six in the morning to six at night.

Then came news that we were about to be posted overseas. I don't know how many times I was being posted overseas, but nothing ever came of it. I'd have loved to go overseas. My mate Eddie Douglas went overseas (he was from Corstorphine), and I often thought how I'd have enjoyed it. But now we were being transferred to a huge camp at a place called Strubby. At that very time, my father died, and so I got let away for the funeral. And then I had to go to Strubby by myself. What a massive place: there was thousands and thousands and thousands of us, all under canvas, and eight to a tent. And we heard that we were going to Okinawa; and we got every different kind of jags for Okinawa.

THE END OF THE WAR

Then this officer came in. He had medals all down his chest, row after row, like a blind; you could have rolled it up. 'You should all be in Okinawa. But the Japs have packed in. The war's finished. It's over!'

What a night. What a night. We had bonfires of everything. We went off our heads. And in due course you handed in your stuff, and you came out with your suit, your hat, your shoes, and your raincoat – you should have seen my suit. George Raft had nothing on me! – and you went to the railway station with all these lads you'd been with. And it was 'All the best, Mac!' and you never seen them again.

I got off the train at Central Station, and I walked down Union Street, carrying my kit-bag. I waited on the white car, the 18. I stood all the way home on it, with my kit-bag beside me. It stopped in Main Street.

I walked up Poplin Street. A lovely feeling, it was. Brilliant. Only Rose and the two girls were in.

WAR AND FAITH

When I was in the RAF I went to every Church Parade. There was those that wouldn't go. If it was an RC Parade they would say they were Church of England, and if it was the other they'd say they were different again. But I was always religious. At home, I always went to church. My father never went to church at all, but he was always one for quoting the Bible. He learned it in the Orange Lodge. In those days in Bridgeton there was a Lodge in almost every street, Landressie Street, West Street, that's Kerr Street now, Mordaunt Street. And he used to go down to Bridgeton Cross and argue with the speakers there. He'd get to the front and argue: he used to speak about trans-substantiation. And we had a family Bible. And my Father left it to me, because he knew me, that I was religious. But oh my. I remember when things were poor I used to get sent to the Pond [*the pawn-shop*] with it. I used to cut through the back – the Pond was in Nuneaton Street. And you'd get about five shillings on it. A piece of oilcloth it used to be wrapped in when I took it. And I've got it at home now; and it's wrapped in that oilcloth yet.

Though I take things very lightly, I can be serious, you see. And faith has always been important to me. And in the war you never got used to what happened, losing people you knew. Dunkirk: I lost a lot of friends there. But the comradeship of the war was the thing. You looked out for each other, you cared about each other. Even now I keep in touch with people.

ARMISTICE

I don't know that I remember the end of the First War. But I remember those Armistice Days. When I was working in the Dye-works you always had the two minutes silence. I've seen us all standing to attention beside the machines. The hooter went, down where the boilers were, and we all stood. My brother, Willie, used to tell me of the atrocities of the trenches, and people thought about that. And my father-in-law got gassed in the trenches, Robert Craig, and he was always ill after that. But as years went on, people forgot.

And I know that in yourself, you over-ran the bad times, took them out of your memory.

There's others, others in the church, would tell you more than I can, that was in the actual fighting. I used to say the only fighting I did in the war was fighting my way into pubs, fighting to get a clean glass. But you had your other side of it. We were just a small work, the Dye-works, about seventy in it. Twelve of us went to the war, and we lost six.

And I'll tell you my worst day. I buried seven in Chester. Seven pilots. I was selected to be on a burial party. 'You, you, and you. Burial Party.' Twelve of us had to go. They had all been shot down. You found them. One in a river, one in a drain. And at the cemetery we carried them one by one. Six of us carried the first. The other six carried the second. And so on. We buried seven pilots that day. And some of their families were there, the ones that lived close perhaps. That was my worst day.

You keep thinking. You have your thoughts every Remembrance. The Youth of your country.

I'm glad for you to tell people this, if you say that it will maybe help people to understand. Because that's what's needed. People need to understand.

From the Castlemilk East Church *Newsletter* of 17th July 1994:

On Tuesday lots of people dropped in at the McCrackens' house. It was their Diamond Wedding anniversary. One of the visitors gave this account to the Newsletter:

    'On the 12th of July 1934 Richard McCracken and Roseanne Craig were married by the Rev. Mr. Sutherland. He was the Minister of the church to which Rose belonged, and where she sang in the choir, St Thomas's in the Gallowgate. They were married in the Manse.

They had known each other since childhood. "Once he stole my whip and peerie," said Rose.

"We couldn't have a celebration of the wedding," said Dick, "because Rose's grandmother had died just 4 or 5 days before the wedding."

"My father said we couldn't celebrate so soon after, but a wee party of us had a tea in the Co-operative tea-rooms," said Rose.

"We went back to Rose's mother's after that," Dick recalled. "I was looking very smart in a silver-grey suit and a silver tie. I'd had to be up early in the morning to get a bath at the steamie."

"I was in a nice pink dress," remembered Rose.

Then they left Rose's mother's house in Nuneaton Street to walk the 5 or 6 minutes to their little kitchen in Poplin Street. They went past the end of Norman Street: there was a big gang of men standing there – the feared gang called "The Norman Conks".

"I thought they might throw something at us," said Rose.

"But I still had my flower in my button-hole," said Dick, "and they gave us a big cheer as we walked by!"

"I got the key of our house from my neighbour, and we let ourselves in. And as you might expect, they'd been at the bed. They'd filled it with peas. You couldn't hear anything for the peas falling on the floor," Rose laughed.

"There must have been three pounds of peas in that bed," laughed Dick. "We could have had pea soup for a week!"

As the conversation neared its end, Dick said quietly, "She's my lassie. I don't know what I'd do without her."'

Blessed with wonderful health, in all his eighty-six years Dick was never once in hospital until the day before he died in 1997.

1996

Mrs Joan Victoria Knox

- An agreement with the United Nations permits Iraq to sell oil, with the proceeds to be used for food and medicine.
- Kofi Annan of Ghana is named Secretary General of the United Nations.
- A gunman opens fire in Dunblane Primary School, killing sixteen children and a teacher, then kills himself.
- Prince Charles and Princess Diana divorce.
- Yasser Arafat is elected President of the Palestinian Authority, taking control of the Occupied West Bank and Gaza.
- The United Nations reports that AIDS is spreading more rapidly: 5.8 million people have died world-wide.

In 1996, Joan Victoria Knox is tall and elegant. She has lived in Castlemilk since it was first built in 1955. Though now eighty-nine years of age, she is a keen swimmer and goes to the swimming baths twice a week. She walks the half-mile to church each Sunday.

━━━━ «◦» ━━━━

I don't like the idea of my name being used. It's not that I'm a particularly private person. But I think that other people had much more difficult experiences of war than I had, than we had, and I don't like being pushed forward. But if you say that you want to use my name … I suppose people who know me would recognise me anyway as soon as you mentioned that my husband's name was Quintin.

CHILDHOOD AND WARTIME: THE FIRST WORLD WAR

I remember the First World War vividly. In fact I remember more about that war than about the Second.

My father was called up in about 1917. He was over thirty by then, and they were having to call up older and older people. He was with the Tank Corps and then the Royal Engineers. He trained in Leith. And when we went over to see him we saw them practicing on the beach. Bayonet practice. I suppose I thought it a kind of joke, seeing them sticking the bayonet into a packed canvas bag. But it was terrible, really; terrible. He spent exactly nine days at the front – it was in France – when he was gassed. They used these poison gas bombs. The gas affected his lungs very badly, and he was in hospital for over a year. They brought him back to England and he was in Grantham. All his life after that he had a lot of chest trouble, though he lived till he was about seventy. Every night he would heat his pillow at the fire before he went to bed. Because if he laid his head on a cold pillow he'd cough all night long.

My mother was in munitions. She left at five in the morning to go off to Singers, and she wasn't home till ten at night. It was the travelling to get there. Some days she wouldn't get her clothes off at all: she'd just lie on the couch in the kitchen in front of the fire. She made the big bombs. Was she a polisher? Or a filler? My aunt and her worked there together, and one was one and the other the other. My mother was really only at home on a Sunday, and I used to have to feed myself, I remember.

I went to school at Battlefield. Yes. Even my school was called a battlefield – one of Mary Queen of Scots's battles, the battle of Langside. The men used to come to the school to do keep-fit exercises, getting ready for the war, I suppose. And a friend's father was killed in the war, Mr Ferguson. But I was just young, and I suppose I didn't fully take it in. And there were other girls, too, whose fathers were killed.

I came from a big family, and lots of the men were in that war. My uncle Danny was drowned, and never found. Another was a prisoner of war – that was Willie. I had an Uncle Johnny in the submarines. Uncle Neil was a plumber and too old to go.

I remember the end of the war. We had a big party at my Gran and Grandpa's house. It was such a relief. And for years afterwards the 11th of November was Armistice Day and everything stopped. I remember if Armistice Day was a school day – I was at Queen's Park – we were taken into the Hall, all assembled there, with Mr Flint, the Headmaster. And at eleven o'clock we all stood in silence for two minutes.

There was dreadful unemployment, then. All sorts of marches and meetings. The soldiers were very angry, very angry indeed. It was a terrible thing to see. We were lucky though. My father had his work all the time, all the way through.

THE SECOND WORLD WAR

I remember all the men in blue: blue trousers, blue jacket, the uniform that the wounded wore. They were all at the hospital in Gilshawhill.

Quintin and I were married in 1935. He was thirty-two and I was twenty-eight.

I was always a church-goer. We went every Sunday to Battlefield West Church in Ledard Road. Sunday School, Guides, Band of Hope. We were guided at the church. My sisters, Winnie and Eunice, were always church-goers too. Am I a religious person? I don't know. I thank God every day for all the blessings. I pray each day at least three times. Is that just because I'm getting old? I don't know. I don't think so, though. And going to church doesn't mean I think I'm good. The church is for sinners. And I feel that God's just letting us loose, to see how we'll do. And what he must think of us silly people I just don't know.

The Second War came as a terrible disappointment. We thought Neville Chamberlain had diverted it. My daughter, Joan, was just three, and we'd moved from Bellgrove Street to Maryhill. Quintin was turned down for the army on medical grounds, and he worked in Insurance and then with Patersons, the music people. But he was in the Home Guard. He was away out in the country, posted in barns on farms, doing guard duty, and he was out a lot. Some just did ARP [Air Raid Precaution] warden duty, and they slept at home. But Quintin came home from work, changed into his uniform, and away out. Every weekend it was, and sometimes midweek as well.

THE BOMBING

When we stayed in Maryhill, the German planes used to come over on their bombing runs. There were three waterways there, the Clyde, the Kelvin and the Canal. and we used to think that must have confused them. For they came over to bomb the shipping. But they never got John Browns. Though they destroyed Clydebank. And they got the tenement building too, next the BBC. That night it was so close to us that our bathroom window was cracked in the blast.

Quintin was out with the Home Guard, and they would go to the bombed building. One time they went into this house, and they were looking for survivors. They heard someone calling 'Help! Help!' but they couldn't see them. They looked away up into the roof, and saw a person perched on a chair, away up in the roof. They must have been blown away up there, but they were still alive and all right.

The Clydebank thing was terrible. We could hear the planes going over, going over, going over. Quintin had to go down there. He told me about it. And there was one little girl running about, looking everywhere for her parents. She was a little Jewish girl. But they never did find her parents. I remember saying to Quintin, 'Could we adopt her?' But he said, 'With this war on I can only take responsibility for my own.'

EVACUATING THE CHILDREN

They were evacuating children from Glasgow away to the country to be safe. Quintin wanted me to take Joan. I said I'd stay, and Joan would go. We had quite a rammy about it. In the end I asked my mother if she'd take Joan, as she was far from the city. Ten weeks she was there with my mother and father. And we went down at the weekend just to let her know she still had a mum and a dad. Then we brought her home. We couldn't put up with her being so far away! We felt we'd panicked, and that we'd be better all being together, that if anything happened we'd all get it.

We had made provision for what we wanted if anything happened to us and Joan survived. For it had happened to so many.

NEIGHBOURS

We stayed in Stratford Street. We had no air-raid shelter there. When the air-raid siren went, we went in to the woman's on the ground floor. Mrs Wallace, Betty. Her husband was in the ARP, and we all went into her house. We put the children in the recess bed in the kitchen with games and things. There would be more than a dozen of us in her house. Sometimes for hours. The night of Clydebank we would be there eight hours. The night of the BBC, maybe six. We thought that the house in the ground floor would be safest. But there was a person, Betty, who was a lodger in the house next to me. She refused point-blank to go into any downstairs house – we lived two-up. She had been bombed out three times in London. Her firm had brought her up to Glasgow, and her three children were evacuated away – she never saw them. She never moved when the air-raid sirens went. She just stayed in her bed.

I stopped working when the war started. I did voluntary nursing in the Western with the Red Cross. It was the civilian population only, there were other hospitals that took the wounded from the forces.

I had cousins in the war, one in the Canadian Army, one in the Air Force. And one cousin was on an oil tanker. It was strange. He had been at Anzio, after the battle there. And he had found a puppy on the Anzio beach, and took it with him. Later, the tanker was hit and all the crew were lost but him, him and his dog. He felt it was something to do with his dog that he was saved.

I remember, too, a neighbour in Ardencraig Quadrant. He had been through all the battles, and never a scratch. But he suffered so terribly in his mind. And there were thousands like him.

FOOD IN THE WARTIME

There never seemed to be a shortage of bread, as it happens. But there was rationing. But that didn't affect us too much. Wages were so low we couldn't afford more anyway.

The coal rationing was terrible. Our coalman came from outside Glasgow, and sometimes he couldn't get in. People used to go with prams to pick up their own coal, and anything else that would burn. We had a gas oven, and I remember that when we hadn't any coal we lit the oven and heated ourselves round the oven.

I don't remember being hungry. Milk was rationed, of course. Meat was rationed. Fish was scarce. But you took a plate to the butchers or the fish shop, because there was no wrapping paper during the war.

When we hadn't the meat, carrot-turnip-onion-potatoes, with a Bovril gravy, was a nice mixture. We used to do something with turnip that made it taste like pineapple. I went to Glasgow Cross for pigs' feet. We made mince with half meat and half lentils to make it stretch. We could do fantastic things with potatoes. Potatoes with milk, mashed potatoes browned under the grill. We washed the skins of onions and boiled them to give some flavour to a soup. It was the winters that were so hard: you needed nourishing food, hot food, to keep you going. Nothing was ever wasted.

We had a radio. I remember when we first got it. I was working in Patersons, and they gave employees a nine-month credit. I paid it up in two months. But it was never switched on till it was paid up. It just sat in the house. And Quintin used to tease me like anything, 'What on earth did you bring it home for?' But that was just me. I wouldn't switch it on till it was paid for. Not like nowadays!

CLOTHING IN THE WARTIME

Clothing was rationed, and you had to make do in all sorts of ways to save your coupons. Quintin used to play cricket, and when we got married he gave it up. I used to make beautiful little dresses for Joan from the white flannel – twenty-two-inches wide.

Then we got flour bags from the grocers – you had to be well in with them to get them. And we washed them and made curtains and pillow-cases out of them.

You could only make plain things, but you weren't going out socially – it was just everyday things you needed. We could get wool, and I used to knit. My mother had trained to be a tailoress, and she'd taught me a few tips. And there was a few neighbours and friends would get together in my house. One night a week we'd get together and work away and pass on tips to each other. They were sad times of course. And some of the women lost their husbands. And with some of the rest of us having our men still at home they got very bitter. Very bitter. It was difficult.

But for all that, Quintin would not go from Patersons into a higher paid job. He wouldn't go to munitions. People made a lot of money in munitions. They were making a bomb. He could have gone. But he said that if he went to munitions the firm he was working with would have trouble getting anyone in his place. So he stayed on with them.

THOUGHTS ON REMEMBRANCE SUNDAY

On Remembrance Sunday, I think that terrible thought of all the young ones that died. The millions in the two World Wars. It's that, that comes back. And of how lucky we were. I always think of a friend of my sister's. A nicer couple you couldn't get. He was a prisoner of war, and spent years in Belsen 2. And although he came home, he needed to go through an operation for something, and died then. I think of my young uncle Danny, too, the one who was drowned and never found. He had just been married before he went off on that voyage.

I think of these two. But I think of them all.

You ask me if I'm a religious person. I wonder. I will not work on a Sunday. I never do a washing on a Sunday. I won't buy messages on a Sunday. I make Sunday a day of rest. I like to set one day aside to think about the things that matter in life.

It's a bit like when I go to the swimming: I love it there when the waves are on: I float, and relax, and let the waves move me. Am I a religious person? What would you say?

THOUGHTS ON WAR AND PEACE

I think God wants us to protect a good way of life, and sometimes that will mean fighting against evil. If you just stood back and did nothing about it, then evil would go on getting away with it.

Fine I remember when the Atom Bomb was dropped. Because it practically ended the war I thought at the time it was all right. Even yet, though, we're hearing about what it did, and people are still suffering and dying from it.

And surely war is always bad. I'm so glad that the big nations are trying to do something about it. But it's terrible that war is still going on.

I pray for peace in my prayers every day.

Although she recently gave up swimming, now in her late nineties Vicky Knox still walks the half-mile to church every Sunday. She lives eighteen floors up in a multi-storey block of flats. Her daughter Joan visits her regularly, coming from the Black Isle, and her grandchildren are grown up with children of their own. One of the founding members of Castlemilk East Church, Vicky taught children in the Sunday School and she has always had a concern for education. After she married, she was never in paid employment. She took care of her parents in their old age and looked after her husband's elderly aunt. In the church's Guild for more than twenty-five years, she was the overseas delegate at the annual Guild Assembly. She spent time in voluntary organisations such as Oxfam, and she took an active interest in politics, helping to found the Conservative Association in Castlemilk. Through her church connection she was in the local committee which established the Castlemilk Community Centre. She still has strong opinions about the way society is developing, and she takes an interest in national politics and international affairs.

1997

Mr Christopher Drummond

- US President, Bill Clinton, and Russian President, Boris Yeltsin, endorse a plan for NATO's expansion into Eastern Europe.
- Princess Diana (born 1960) is killed in a car accident in France. Her death and funeral are the occasion of widespread expressions of grief.
- The Research Unit at Roslin, Midlothian, announce that they have cloned a sheep. They name it Dolly.
- The film *Titanic* is released. It will become the all-time biggest money-maker in film history, earning over $1.8 billion world-wide.

In 1997, Mr Christopher Drummond is a keen bowler, playing on grass in the summer and on indoor rinks in winter. He and his wife Sadie spend a lot of time with the family.

MY EARLY DAYS WITH MY FAMILY

I was born in 1922. I don't think my father was in that first war. I don't think he was in the Army. But I don't know. No-one ever spoke of it. He was an Inspector with the Cleansing Department, in the Depot in Haghill. He died when I was just four-year-old. That was a good job in those days I suppose, with the Cleansing. He originally came down from the Highlands, Ardrishaig. I was sent up there when my father died, to get me out the road. In they days, the coffin was in the house.

We stayed at Parkhead, in Palace Street. I never remember any talk of the war, not even when I was at school. I went to Newlands School. It's closed now of course. And then to Riverside. It's gone too: demolished.

I can remember my father when I was a four year old. I remember sitting on his knee trying to straighten his pinkie. He'd the same trouble as I have with my hands. They say it's hereditary. There's the operations I've had on them. No one can tell you how *he* got it, of course. He would take me to the pictures, too. And he took me to Ibrox too, some afternoons. And on the way back he'd go in to Flynns on the corner, 'For a paper', he said it was. I know now what it was he went in for, of course!

I had three sisters, all much older than me. And so my mother went out to work. They gave her a job in the Cleansing Department in Haghill after my father died, washing the towels for the men, and cleaning the Inspectors' offices. The sisters was Lizzie, Maisie, and then Isa. When my father died, I used to turn to my oldest sister's man, he kind of took the place of my father, Lizzie's man. He's still alive, ninety-three he is; Jimmy. Jimmy Fisher.

MY SISTERS AND THEIR MEN

My youngest sister, Isa, got very badly burned with a wee electric fire. She was working as a nanny to these people who had twins. They were up at their holiday house, up near Stirling. And this day Isa was standing in front of this fire when her apron caught fire. She was in a bad way in Stirling for a long time. I never went through to see her. I was too young. But Jimmy went through. I remember her getting it all treated. She was burned all up to her face. Her face was all right though. But she was very badly burned. She always wore a silk scarf to hide it. She got a job as a domestic at the Royal, and when she went to work there she knew all the professors, and one of the professors talked her into getting skin grafts.

Her man was in the Second War. He stayed round the corner, and we used to go to things together. He was a labourer and he got called up. He was in the Airborne Division, and he went into Arnhem. He wasn't a paratrooper, he went in in one of the gliders. And he was posted missing. It was a worrying time. We heard he'd been taken prisoner. You'll have heard of Lord Haw Haw – he gave his name and number out over the radio from Germany. I think it was the only night my mother hadn't listened to him, and I remember someone coming up to her door to tell her that night. Tommy Maxwell: he was wounded, but he didn't lose any limbs or that, but he was a prisoner.

Lizzie's husband was a special constable, and he stayed at home. Jimmy evacuated his three children out of Glasgow. He built a wee hut on a farm two miles beyond East Kilbride, and so he kept them there.

Maisie's husband was a turner in Beardmores like myself. So he never went to the war either.

MY WORKING LIFE: AN ENGINEER IN THE WAR EFFORT

From Riverside School I went as a van boy with Beatties Bakery up in Paton Street in Dennistoun. From six in the morning to six at night. It was a horse-drawn van. You'd to be in early to load up the fancy stuff, and then it was off to Paisley Road Toll, Rutland Crescent, Blackburn Street, delivering to all the wee shops, the wee dairies as we used to call them. You'd leave twelve loafs one day, and get nine back the next: people had no money. It was all dockers and there might be no work that week. After a year and a half, I went to Wyllie and Lochheads wallpaper department, tying up wallpaper. Then I went to Beardmores after that.

I served my apprenticeship as a fitter. It was poor wages for five years. We did twelve hour shifts. The tradesmen were all on bonus, so they'd not much time to teach you the trade. They're not going to stop and mess about trying to teach you when they've their bonus to make. So mostly you had to teach yourself. But you were working to help the war effort. It was intricate work, working to thou's of an inch, to very precise limits. And so you had to do it well, and you thought, 'This is part of the war effort'.

Beardmores were making guns for battleships. I worked on 3.7 or 4.7. Not the armour plating, but the mechanism. I worked on the mechanism, the lever for opening the breech to put the shell in. It was on the breech-block that I worked, and then you'd see the gun going off to get the armour plating and the turrets put round them. Across the road they made the 16-inch guns. The barrels were made there, and they rifled them on huge turning lathes. Highly skilled stuff. There was various other things, including 25-pounders for tanks. I don't know why they were called 25-pounders. But they were for the tanks.

There were the air raids, of course. Just the usual air raids. And you'd have to go to the shelters. In Beardmores, when it was night shift, you'd to go to Rigby Street. But eventually you weren't leaving the factory at all. It was the war effort and you just had to get on with it. Beardmores itself was never hit. The nearest bomb to fall was in Allan Street. I remember going down there to see it the next day.

I met Sadie in Beardmores, too. I was at this bench, then there was a passage, and Sadie worked across at a milling machine.

Beardmores went right up to the Shettleston Road – the armour-plating works was there. There was a train ran in to Beardmores bringing the steel. As the war progressed, they built a tunnel under Duke Street so as people going from one side to the other could go straight there. They'd found that when they'd to go out and across the road, some of the labourers were dodging off to the pub. That stopped all that.

In the war they hushed things up a wee bit, what ships was getting sunk and all that, so you never knew. But after a while they'd stock-piled enough of these naval guns. Then they just sent for you and told you were being transferred. So off I went to Harland and Wolffs, by train from Whitby Street to Scotstoun. And I worked on putting the turrets round the guns. I worked on shore. But sometimes they sent two fitters out with the ships if they were going on trials. I was to go one time, but the plan was changed.

RESERVED OCCUPATION AND WAR SERVICE

When you worked in armaments you were a reserved occupation. That meant you didn't get called up into the Army. But I remember feeling a wee bit embarrassed at not being called up.

I had friends got called up early in the war. From the next close, there was a chap that was at school with me. Gilbert McArthur. He came from Islay, and couldn't even speak English when he first arrived, only the Gaelic. He worked with the railway, delivering with a horse and cart. He became a paratrooper, and he got killed in Italy. I saw him a couple of times when he was home on leave. Then I never saw him again. 'Gilbert's missing,' someone would say. I remember he was listed as missing, presumed killed. It seems these paratroopers had been dropped before they were over the land. The story was that the American pilots had wanted to get away again before they came in range of the guns. But you never know if the stories are true.

But you do feel embarrassed when you're at home, and other mothers have their sons away. It was like that with Tommy Maxwell, my sister Isa's man. He was in the Royal Artillery, stationed in Britain, getting leave every three months. He got fed up with people saying, 'Is this you home *again*?' So even though he was stationed in Dungeness, and being bombed right, left and centre, people seeing him here thought he was getting away with it. That was what made him join the Airborne Division.

Certainly, I was supposed to go. I went to the St Mungo Halls for my Medical for the Fleet Air Arm. But it was a couple of years before they called me up.

After it's all by you realise how lucky you've been. Now I feel I was lucky to be in a reserved occupation, even though it embarrassed me so much at the time.

OFF TO THE WAR

When I got my papers, I never gave a thought to fighting or possibly dying. When I went off to the war I don't think my mother shed a tear. But yes, I expect Sadie did. I had to go to Aberdeen, Bridge of Don. Six weeks in Aberdeen, ten weeks in Edinburgh. It was all right. I didn't really give it a lot of thought.

I had embarkation leave, and then I went back to Edinburgh, this big garage, a big shed, with all the beds in it. About midnight they shouted out the names, and that was you off to wherever. I suppose it was so you couldn't tell anyone. It was only when you got there that you realised where you were going. Of course by then you were a Cameron Highlander. Why I was a Cameronian I don't know. I'd always said, I hope I never have to wear one of they tammys. But once you left Aberdeen that was you a Cameron Highlander: a big tammy and a kilt.

It was very near the end of the war. We crossed the channel to Calais, and got a train down through France to Austria and then to Italy, to Trieste at the top of the Adriatic. It was very busy. The Yugoslavs were wanting Trieste and the Allies wouldn't give it to them. I was on the border post on guard duty. It was certainly called active service. For me that just meant that you got to send your letters home for free. You just wrote on the envelope, 'Active Service', and the letters were sent home free of charge. They kept us busy, with exercises and drills. And I know Sadie told you that I won the competition for the best equipped soldier.

I was in Italy when the Hiroshima bomb went off. We were staying in Polo. We were staying in this big building. It had been a hospital. We were making to go home eventually, but just as we were about to leave, the Yugoslavs closed the roads, and so they had to bring in a big boat to take us all off. And we sailed to Treviso and were kept in a transit camp until such times as we got home.

THOUGHTS OF FAITH

When I came home I never went back to the engineering. I got a temporary job for six months with the Co-operative Bakery in McNeill Street, and I was there for twenty-seven years. Some temporary job!

My mother had always been a great church-goer, every Sunday she went. And so I was always involved in the church. I was in the BB in Newlands East Church on the London Road, the 228 Glasgow Company. Later I went to the Queen Mary Street BB. The man in the top flat was the Captain, and he must have talked me into it. I used to go the church parades in the Army. Sometimes it was in actual churches, but other times it was just in a big shed with a padre.

I've been glad that my own three sons have never had to go to war.

I knew that that atom bomb was out of the ordinary: you saw the pictures, the devastation. I know it was terrible, but there'd have been millions more killed if the war there had gone on. It nipped the war in the bud.

I don't know if these things are in the hands of God. I think that's too much to say. I don't know if God has thoughts about war. I don't know the answer to that. I remember going to a church fellowship, and a professor explaining about the Polaris missiles. He was pointing out that they were a deterrent, and that if we had them others wouldn't start a war against us. There was a balance which would keep the peace.

I think war happens because the powers that be decide 'We're going to war'. Right now they're sitting round the table in Ireland. But will they cure the man in the street?

THOUGHTS ON REMEMBRANCE SUNDAY

I always like to go to the Remembrance Sunday Service. In the silence I think of Tommy Maxwell.

And I think more of the First World War, of the trenches and all the men who died. I believe that in the days when I was at school the traffic all stopped at eleven o'clock on Remembrance Day.

I've always thought that there was nothing very interesting in my experiences of the war. But now I look at it, maybe there is.

———— «◈» ————

It was characteristic of Mr Drummond, 'Christie', as his wife Sadie called him, not to regard his experience of war as of much interest to others. For he was a very quiet, modest man. His long unbroken service with the bakery illustrated his readiness to play his part in long-term low-profile activity. He enjoyed sitting in company, but he was a listener rather than a speaker. He was very proud of their family, their sons and their grandchildren. Their three sons all made their mark in different ways. None served in the armed forces, although the eldest, an engineer like his father, spent some time in the Royal Fleet Auxiliary. After returning to life ashore that son worked with Rolls Royce, writing the service manuals for their jet engines until his death at the age of fifty. Christie and Sadie enjoyed retirement, and continued their involvement with a local bowling club. Sadie died in 2003, and Christie looked after himself at home, though constantly under the kindly eye of his sons and their families. Early in 2004, Christie himself died peacefully at home.

1998

Mrs Cecilia McQuade

- Iraq's Saddam Hussein refuses to allow United Nations weapons inspectors into various installations.
- US cruise missiles strike alleged training complexes in Afghanistan, aimed at killing Osama bin Laden.
- In Northern Ireland, a car-bomb detonated by the Real IRA in Omagh kills twenty-eight people and injures over 200.
- US President, Bill Clinton, admits to 'inappropriate relationship' with former White House intern Monica Lewinsky.
- Terrorist bombs explode at US Embassies in Nairobi, Kenya and Dar-es-Salaam, Tanzania, killing over 100 people and injuring over 1,000.
- Cloned sheep 'Dolly' gives birth to a lamb.
- US and UK continue air strikes against Iraq.
- Good Friday Agreement sets up new Northern Ireland Assembly.

**In 1998, Mrs Cecilia McQuade is a member of the Pensioners'
Action Group, and with the history group there has recently
taken part in a radio programme about children's games
and street-songs from her childhood days.**

CHILDHOOD AFTER THE FIRST WORLD WAR

I don't want you to use my name, now. I don't want people knowing who I am. Oh well. I suppose you're right. If they hear my husband's name was Bernard, and that my name's Cecilia, they'll know soon enough that I'm Celia McQuade. Yes, then. You'll have to use my name.

I was called after my Granny, Cecilia Hodge Craig. But she always said I wasn't. My mother must hae been the sort that didn't like a lot of names. She only gave me two of her names. My Granny wanted me to have it all. But she was Cecilia Selkirk Wilson Reid Hodge. Imagine being Cecilia Selkirk Wilson Reid Hodge Craig. Imagine that name on your ration book.

My Granny was the daughter of a seventh daughter, and there was a wee bit of a charm in her. You know how, when children were ill, my Granny was called for, and she would make up potions for them. I was born in Camlachie, up near Celtic Park. It was East Hope Street, and then they changed it to Holywell Street. The Camlachie School was there.

I'm eighty-three now, the 17th of September. I was born in 1915. The other war was on. My father wasnae away in the war. He was a coalman, worked with the coal. My uncles was in the war. My mother's brothers was in it. But they all came home. There was three of them. They stayed with my Gran. And it was her I was reared wi'. You see, my mother died when she was twenty-six, and left three of us. I was brought up wi my Granny. My father lived there too. We stayed in East Hope Street. My Granny had a house up the one stair, and my mother had had a house two closes down. I remember I was taken up to the hospital to see my mother in Duke Street hospital with my Auntie Maggie. I mind o' going up to see her. It was during the bad flu that was out then. My father caught it, and then my mother took it, and she died.

I was at her funeral. She was buried in Janefield Cemetery. My chum, Cathy, she lost her mother too. We'r Sunday afternoon was going to Janefield and then on to Dalbeth. We used to go the midden at the cemetery and pick all the flowers out. You know how people maybe took fresh flowers and put them on the grave, and the others they'd put in the midden but they'd be all right. And we'd put all the good flowers on their graves, my mother in Janefield, her mother in Dalbeth. A lot of time we spent in the cemeteries I can assure you of that.

My Granny had us all together in the room and kitchen. My Uncles and all of us. There was three of us. But my brother died just before my mother, the youngest one. He took ill and died. But my Mother didnae know he'd died, for they didnae tell her. He was William. I was just six when she died. I was the oldest. There was me and Robert and then William, the one that died. I just faintly remember William. My Granny had him there with us while my mother was in the hospital. My mother was the oldest of my Granny's family.

One Uncle kept very close to my mother, and when he was away at the war he used to write a lot to my mother and sent her wee souvenir things, wee fancy cards, wi' embroidery on them. The flags were on them, done in beautiful embroidery. He used to send them from France, to tell her he was all right. In fact it's no' long since I done away wi' them. In fact it broke my heart to have to get rid of them when I came here.

You see, my father had a lot of brothers too. They were in the war too. I think he had three brothers in it. They were all spared. But you never heard them talking about the war. In my days, children were seen and not heard. If there was any conversations going on you wernae supposed to listen. They were a crowd in Camlachie, the Craigs. Everyone knew them in Camlachie. The Craigs. And the Hodges. My Granny Hodge had seven sons and two daughters. My Granny Craig had about five or six. They came from Ireland. My grandfather was born and buried out the same house, they'd stayed in Camlachie that long. There was a stable in Gill's Court. There was a contractor's there, Hodges. All my people were carters, and you took horses for granted.

We used to go to the Carter's Mission and to the Coalhill Street Mission – that was the City Mission. They had Sunday School and the Band o' Hope at night. My Granny had went to the Carter's Mission. I went over there myself wi my pals. I was a great one for the Missions. I used to go over to the Missions at night. And on a Sunday I'd go to St Thomas's in the Gallowgate.

I went to Camlachie School. My mother had a sister, only about three years older than me. She went to school with us as well.

THE BIG QUESTIONS OF LIFE

My mother died when she was twenty-six, and her brothers and her sisters lived on. And I had an Uncle died when he was nearly ninety, and he'd no family. I mean, many's the time you sat and thought about it. And they were all quite good ages when they died. My Granny was eighty-nine or something. And you used to look back and say, 'How was my mother taken at twenty-six?' I must be honest. I really used to go to the church a lot. I'm no saying this just for praise or anything like that. If ever I was up against it, and I was up against it quite a lot. Because you miss your mother. There's different things, as you go through life, that you need your mother. And that's when it hits you. Because my Granny was there but it doesn't matter how good anybody is to you, you always miss them. And many's the time if I hadnae had the church ... That's why I keep saying the noo, 'I don't know what the young yins'll do when they've nothing to hold on to.' For the church was a great consolation to me. And I used to feel, when I came oot, that well, I could face things again.

Even all through my life I've had to dae that, many's the time.

You see, my Father got married again, when I was twelve. And he wanted us to go with him, and the step-mother wanted us tae. But my Granny wouldn't let us go. She said she'd made a promise to my mother to look after us. I always kept in touch wi' my Dad. And he never neglected us, and he used to clothe us. And I used to have to go to him and say, 'Sonny's needin' socks.' And my step-mother would say, 'Can they not be darned?' and I'd say, 'My Granny says, "No".' 'Sonny's needin' shoes.' 'Can they no' be mended?' – I was in the middle – 'My Granny says, "No".' It was hard going on me. I was the go-between!

But I'll tell you one thing. I never wanted. Because there was never anyone came and gave me it, but The Good Man always made sure I had the opportunity to work for it. And I can honestly say that if I wanted for anything, I never got it handed to me on a platter. But something turned up, and I got work. I used to work in the American Bar, the ice-cream shop in the Gallowgate. Half-a-crown I got for working the whole day on a Saturday.

ARMISTICE DAY IN THE 1920s

You know how they hold Armistice Day on a Sunday, Remembrance Sunday? Well, when I was at school it was always on the 11th of November. And on Armistice Day you always went in your uniform to school. I was in the Girl Guides. That was the only day you'd go to school in your uniform. You had to stand to attention in your class when the two minutes' silence came, standing at the side of your desk. There was boys in their BB uniforms, Scouts, Guides. And teachers too.

There was silence all over. Even all the traffic stopped.

And there was always children in the class who'd lost their Dads, or someone else belonging to them. And in that two minutes' silence there was a lot of people got upset. You'd see them in tears. You knew they'd lost somebody.

LEAVING SCHOOL AND STARTING WORK

I left school at fourteen, and went into the McCord's Mill, off the Gallowgate, at the bottom of Millerston Street. I worked there for a couple of months just. I was caught in one of the machines. I was going by and I got caught in it. It was the spinners, and my frock was torn off me. If I hadnae been quite strong at the time it might have been worse. But I was all right. It was in the weaving sheds. The big weaving machines. The bobbins was all spinning, and my clothes was just drawn intae it. And I'd to pull myself out, and it was lucky that someone came and could turn it off. I could have got badly hurt. But I survived it anyway! I tell you again. The Good Man was watching me. There's so much 'Ifs', and I just seemed to escape it all the time.

I left it and went into the shirt factory, Zeniths, near Abercrombie Street. I was an ironer. I got the offer of being a cutter, but I couldnae afford to take it for I wouldnae have enough wages to gie my Granny. There were better prospects, but you took less wages to start. So I couldnae dae it. I'd to stay an ironer, stayed an ironer for ten years, nearly till I was married.

MARRIAGE AND WAR-TIME

Bernard and I had met first through a wee Rambling Club. We used to go hiking, rambling at the weekend. This wee crowd from the Bluevale Street organised it, and Bernard was from Bluevale Street. We'd all get the tramcar to Millerston and walk out to Cumbernauld up to Lily Loch. We got engaged the night my brother, Robert, got married – Bernard asked my Dad that night if he could marry me – and we were married in the June. The war had started on the 3rd of September, Bernard's birthday. He was expecting to be called up, so we just got married. We were married in the manse of St Thomas's by the minister, Mr Sutherland. That was the church that the McCrackens went to, Mr McCracken that died not long ago. But Bernard wisnae called up, because he worked in the Forge, in the steelworks, Beardmores. And he wore glasses so that was against him. But he was in the Home Guard – and he used to say he was the only one who never retreated!

My brother, Robert, was in the war. He was in the tanks, a driver he was. He must have been twenty-one when he went in. And the day we were married, the 14th of June, they had Dunkirk. He was at that thingmy at Dunkirk. He hurt his back but he got home, came back on one of they wee boats. Then he was back over. He was in the tanks in France, and on across the Rhine into Germany. He came back safely.

At that time I was working in a baker's shop, the Co-operative in Dalmarnock Road. We all had to take our turn at fire-watching in the bakery at night. Nicol Mairs. You stayed out all night. We were there when we were needed.

THE BOMB AT ALLAN STREET

When the bomb landed in Allan Street, Bernard was working in the power station in Dalmarnock Road. They saw the bomb coming, and they thought it was going to land on the power station. And I always remember how he came in that night, I'll never forget it. He said they got flat doon, and the earth shook as it hit Allan Street just on the other side of the road. It only missed the power station by a street. It was terrible.

I remember it too. We were in the shelter. We'd to go to the shelter, across the road in Ardenlea Street. You just had to rise and run when the siren went. The sound of it was deafening. You were expecting bombs at that time, but you just didn't know what it was, what had happened. There must have been about twenty of us in the shelter, children as well as old ones. I hadnae any children yet, but I was pregnant then. I was expecting my first baby. I lost it.

But everyone got a terrible fright that night of the bomb. And the next day I had four budgies to watch. For anybody that had anybody went away and stayed with them. They'd all got such a fright. It cleared the place for a few nights. But I'd nowhere to go tae, I just had to stay. So they all left their budgies wi' me, and I'd four of them tae watch.

EVACUATED TO ABERDEEN

I was evacuated away to Aberdeen in the end, up at Lord Aberdeen's estate. Haddo House. It was the place that pregnant mothers were taken to. They evacuated us, a crowd of women. Lord Aberdeen used to have a service every morning. You should have seen us all, trailing in to the service. It was a lovely place. But I lost the baby up there in the May, the 14th of May. He was due. Toxaemia of pregnancy they said. But it was the shocks. The bomb and that – the whole system was upset. It all worked inwardly. He was a wee boy. I gave him the name Henry. I think if I hadnae been up there I wouldnae have got over it the way I did, for everyone was so kind. The attention you got and everything. I thought of him through the years. And I nearly got killed going back to see his grave. He was buried up at Tarves in Aberdeen. We were going up to visit his grave when we were in a car smash that weekend. I was sitting in the front of the car, and I ended up in the hospital in Montrose. So we never got to see it.

When I lost the baby I kept asking, 'How did it happen to me?' Something like that could either make or mar you. There I was in Aberdeen, lost my baby. And there was another girl there who didn't even want to *see* her baby – just wanted it adopted away. You ask, 'Why?' And you think, 'This is sent to try you.'

I was really lucky that I turned to the church for guidance. I've met in with good people, but somehow or other it was things you couldn't talk about you had to go and think about. And the church was one of the places you got thinking.

MUNITIONS WORKER IN THE HOME GUARD

Bernard expected to get called up. But because he worked at the Forge they never took him. It was a reserved occupation. They produced the shells for the guns, the ammunition, and I suppose it would be the steel for the ships and the tanks. Bernard worked in the boilers, for the steam presses. So he never got called up. But he was dying to get away. He wanted to be into the war, like all the rest of them. But it was the Home Guard for him.

He'd be called out at night. If there was a fire they'd be called out. He'd be out sometimes two and three nights a week. And even after a night when you'd been called out you still had to go to your work next morning.

THE END OF THE WAR

It was a great feeling when the war ended, and you knew everything was finished. We had a radio in our house in Ardenlea Street, and we heard it on the radio. We'd a party when my brother, Robert, came home, in his place in the London Road. He had a wee boy and a wee girl then, and he'd been away a while.

Then we heard about the Atom bomb. You couldn't believe it, when it happened. You knew it was more than just another bomb. I knew it was more severe, more danger in it. But you know it's not God's doing, God's no' to blame. It's man's inhumanity to man,

Then you're raising your own family, Craig, Bernard, and Celia. And you prayed that they'd never have to go to war. Craig did join the paratroops, and I went daft. He joined with his friend Gil Nicoll

– they were in the Youth Fellowship at the church together, with Russell Clarkson. And when they were doing their first jump they never told me about it till it was well over.

And here I am now. They've all done well.

———— «◇» ————

Cecilia McQuade has lived in Castlemilk since 1955. Her three children have all grown up and married. One lives in the East of Scotland, one in England, and one in Canada, and there are grandchildren and great-grandchildren. Celia, as she is called by friends, looked after her husband through a long illness until his death in 1979. She herself had to fight her way back to health in 1990 after being attacked by a thief in the lift of her multi-storey flats. She was thrown to the floor of the lift and robbed.

She has now moved to a sheltered-housing complex. In 2003, two of her children organised a surprise 88th Birthday Party for her, inviting the other residents of the Complex. A small live band played a wide range of songs, and a number of the guests sang songs they liked. For the meal her family had chosen Celia's favourite party menu: hot pie and peas, followed by cream scones and dumpling.

1999

Mr Alfred Hamilton

- NATO begins air strikes against Serbia.
- Britain completes its destruction of its stocks of anti-personnel mines.
- Russia moves military forces against Chechnya.
- Two Libyans suspected of the Lockerbie bombing are tried in the Netherlands in a specially constituted Scottish Court.
- Berlin becomes the capital of Germany for the first time since the Second World War.
- Michelangelo's Sistine Chapel paintings are revealed in a new brightness following cleaning.
- The MacPherson enquiry into the death of black teenager Stephen Lawrence finds the police guilty of 'institutional racism'.
- On 1st July the Scottish Parliament is officially opened. (59% of the electorate voted on 12th May 1999.)

In 1999, Mr Alfred Hamilton and his wife Mary now live in a quiet street in Castlemilk. Once or twice a week Alfie meets friends from his former work with the Glasgow Subway.

THE YOUNG DAYS

Before I say anything, I'll let you into my room, and I'll show you some ancient history. You try to forget these things. They're in the past. But you still have to sleep at night. I was only twenty when I was called up.

I stayed in Todd Street, and I used to work in the Blochairn Steelworks, by the Garngad, 'the Good and the Bad'. And, yes, I was only twenty when I was called up. There was two of us called up at the same time, and we finished up in Morpeth together, in the Queen's Own Cameron Highlanders. I'd a brother, Geordie, and my brother, Andy, was ten years older. My father, Old Geordie, he wasn't in the First World War, because he worked in the steelworks. (He died in 1945, just as the Second War ended, and I came home from Palestine on compassionate leave to see him.)

In Beardmores, I remember, they used to have a Cadet Force. It was made up from the young lads that worked there, young boys sixteen and seventeen. They went into the Regular Army when they were of age. When *I* was a lad, I just used to chase the lassies! I was a great cyclist, too. Five or six of us would go off, down to Dumbarton and away up to Loch Awe. They Scottish Youth Hostels were great. It was just a shilling [5 *pence*] and another thruppence [1 *pence*] for a nice white sheet. You'd go off with your pals all Saturday and Sunday, and then be ready for your work on the Monday.

My first job was in the tannery, with my uncle, in Duke Street. The hides used to come in the gate in a horse and cart, all piled high. The hides came from the docks – they'd come from Argentina, mostly. They came in and were taken up to the Beam Shed, where they put acid on the hides to soften them. Then they put them through to take the hair all off them.

When we were young, we used to run about the Mission Halls in the Gallowgate. The greatest one was Dr Cossar's Mission. It was just a wee place next the 'Saracen Heid', the 'Sarry'. On a Saturday, we got hot peas. Mr Lee taught us stories, and Mrs Lee played the piano for the songs.

On a Sunday, my faither would take four of us to the church, St Thomas's in the Gallowgate. There was seven of us in the family. There was Andrew and George and me – I got called Alfred after my mother's brother; and there was the girls, Jean, May, Betty and Elizabeth, yes one called Betty, and one called Elizabeth, I don't know why.

In the steelworks, I worked an overhead crane, a five-tonner. Then I came down to work beside my faither in the mill. He was what you called a 'breaker-doon', in the melting shop.

CALL-UP

I was not long twenty when I got called up. The papers came in mid-December in 1941. Doon I went to Charing Cross. On the 15th of January, I got my papers and a travel warrant, and off to Morpeth. There we drilled and drilled. We were just twenty-two miles across the sea from Gerry, and at the time the Gerry U-boats was sinking all our boats. That initial training was to bring you to be a full-fledged soldier. After you'd passed your Proficiency Test your pay went up from seven shillings to fourteen shillings.

I was sent then to Ringway in Manchester, to the 7th Queen's Own Cameron Highlanders, the 7th Battalion, 'The Shiny Seventh' we were called. And all the talk was, 'We want to get this war finished.' And this General Browning came from the Middle East to give us a talk. And it was him was going to start a new Regiment, 'The Parachutists'. That's what we were called, then. None of your 'Paratroopers'. No. 'Parachutists' we were. Well this General Browning, he gave us the notion to join, and that was the last we saw of him. Though there's now a Browning Barracks in Aldershot.

Well, in the Paras we were all friends, officers and men all on the one level. Before you jumped from a plane you did your training. There was two or three aircraft hangers, like a big gym. You'd learn to swing from a frame, then you'd learn dropping doon. There was an aircraft fuselage in the hanger, and you'd all get in the fuselage. There was an aperture in the floor. There was a red light and then the green light and you stepped forward and dropped through. We had the Whitley bomber, with that aperture. Then the Yanks brought the DC7, the Dakota. It had the door. That was magic, for you just stepped out the door. With dropping through the aperture, if you didn't get it just right you'd catch your face as you went – hit your nose on the edge – 'Ring the Bell', as we said. There was a few times people rang the bell.

I was very fit. I never hurt myself once in a jump. To get your wings you had to do so many jumps. After you'd learned from the fuselage in those hangers, you had to jump from aircraft. You did five drops from a plane, including one night drop, and three from balloons. With the balloons you'd go up higher and higher, tethered to the ground, and then you just had to go over the side.

OFF TO WAR

We knew we'd soon be sent to war, but we didn't know where to. And in your mind you're asking, 'Am I going to come back?'

We got twenty-seven days' embarkation leave, before leaving for a secret destination. We got on to a ship in Glasgow, and we went down to Sandbank. Then they opened the chains that was across the Clyde to keep the U-boats out, and we were off, shouting 'Cheerio, Glesca!' You never knew where you were going. You looked out of your ship and all you could see all round was the edge of the world, all round you. But all the time you were being fed with pills for dysentery, pills for malaria. In the end we came to land. It was as if you came down-hill coming in, down off the sea. We landed in Iran, and we went to Sousse next, all set in wee tents. I remember a monsoon came and washed everything away.

They took us to North Africa, and before we were taken into the line they kept us training, training. Round Tobruk and Benghazi, they had a lot of empty villages. The Arabs had all gone south and left the villages. We practised dropping into these villages, practised avoiding snipers, occupying the villages. We were fully equipped, with all that to carry. And you're not daft. All this training's not for nothing. You know you're going to meet opposition and you know you're going to fight them.

We had a Regimental Band. Of course they didn't spend all their time playing tunes. When they weren't playing or practising they used to pack the chutes. You'd go to collect a chute, and the guy would say, 'There. That's a blanket in there.' And it would be in your mind all the time – 'Is that really a chute, or *is* it a blanket?' When you were jumping, though, you never forgot how you learned to do it first: 'Keep your feet together and your knees together and you'll meet Mother Earth as you should.'

But for us, there was no action in North Africa. But some of the divisions of the Paras were taken across from North Africa to drop near Mount Etna in Sicily. The ones that came back were in a terrible condition, they said it was hell. The ack-ack was terrible, and they were being *shoved* out the plane by the Jump Master. There was a stick of twenty to twenty-five men and you weren't allowed to stop, just one after the other you had to go. Five of you, then your equipment, then five of you, then your equipment. You just had to keep going. But these lads had had it bad. And they were keeping us in reserve for the next incident.

ITALY

The cruiser, *Dido*, took us across from North Africa to Taranto, in the heel of Italy. We fought our way up through Italy, through Bari and Rimini. And then we were held at Cassino for six months. We were bombed day and night there. We were just fighting as infantry at that time. I was a first-class soldier. We had to dig in. We dug a hole and that was where we lived for months. Two of us lived in that hole. And from up on Monte Cassino, Gerry could see everything. But you just took things as they came. After six months outside Cassino, we got all our cla'es de-loused. We'd been in them for months, with nae bath, nothing. The shells went on and on. But you had to keep humorous about it or you'd get bomb-happy. We'd sit in our trenches at night. And you'd hear Gerry bringing up the mechanised artillery. There was one we called 'The Sobbin' Sisters'. That was the worst. It fired six at a time. And they made that sobbin' sound when you heard them going. And you never knew where they'd land.

PARACHUTE DROP

With our red berets we had quite a name. We served under a General Scobie, and we were known as 'Scobie's Butchers'. We were taken over to Greece, and we dropped supplies by plane to the Resistance there. You'd drop the supplies out the door. But you always had your own chute on, in case the case of supplies pulled you out through the door. It happened sometimes. Then they dropped us into Salonika.

You never knew what you were going into when you dropped. But by the time we got there, we found that Ellas had chased the Germans further north. So we marched down from Salonika to Athens, and we saw the tanks coming off the boats into Athens, with the sea-borne landing.

There was the time we dropped into Toulouse and Marseilles in Southern France. We dropped into German-occupied territory. We were to prepare to build a bridge across a river. The Germans had got word we were coming. They'd got word that there would be gliders coming in, so they had filled the field with poles, great huge poles in the ground, in the field where they knew the gliders would be landing. The gliders went in before us. What a mess they were in. Smashed to pieces.

We always dropped in the moonlight, so the enemy couldn't see us.

And we never knew where we were going to land.

That night we dropped under fire. As you came down you heard the bullets whizzing by, artillery shells whistling past you. When we landed, two of us, Jock Sneddon and me, we saw a farmhouse, and we went over and battered the door. The woman was terrified. But when she heard we were Scottish, she sat us down and gave us a glass of wine. Then Jock and I went to find our Unit.

Aye. All that. It was good and it was bad.

THOUGHTS OF FAITH

I told you about the wee Missions when I was growing up. That Dr Cossar's one. Dr Cossar would take boys that were good Christians off for weekends. And at the Mission you'd get asked if you wanted to be converted. And he'd give you all a lecture. He lived in Monteith Row, and at weekends he'd take you off to his farm. 'Ragamuffins, here we come!' It was good. You'd get tea and a big piece and jam.

It all goes through my mind at times. In the Army, you went to Church parades. And then that time I got two weeks' compassionate leave at the end of the war. And then, after my father died, I was moved to the Isle of Wight. I thought I was getting demobbed, but they sent us over to Palestine. I didn't want to go there. I wanted to go home. But we stayed in Gaza, and there would be times we went up to Tel Aviv.

ARMISTICE

But as for Armistice Day. In the Army we held our own Armistice Day, in the Isle of Wight I remember it. But since then, well, I've never bothered going to a Parade. No. I tell a lie. I did once go, when there was some of them went from the British Legion up the road. We went to Croftfoot and we got sausage rolls. But just the once. When I worked in the Corpy – in the Subway – and there's something. I came through the war without a scratch, but I got a broken neck and all sorts from the General Public in peacetime.

When I was in the Subway, they picked people to go in their uniform to the Parade. But not me. It's only the 'big boys' that get you over to march about. And then they go wining and dining.

On Armistice Day, I just sit about. Yes, I lost a lot of people I knew. But that's another story.

You were losing them every day.

I think of them.

Now you can go through and see my wee museum. My medals, the photos. My history. It's all there, on the walls.

And I'll go and make you a cup of tea. What do you take in it?

———— ««»» ————

When he was demobbed at the end of the war, Alfie Hamilton returned to his work at the Blochairn Steelworks. When it closed, he joined the Glasgow Corporation Transport, first as a tramcar conductor, then as a tram driver. His conductress was Mary Dick, and they married in 1955. Alfie then spent fifteen years as a bus driver, and later worked on the Glasgow Subway. When the Subway

closed for renovation, he became the gate-man at the Sunblest bakery in Parkhead until he retired.

Their three children were all connected with the Army. Their eldest son, Alfred, served twelve years with the Royal Highland Fusiliers, with two tours of duty in Northern Ireland. He now lives with his family in New York, USA. Their son, John, spent several years in the Territorials. And their daughter, Mary, worked in the NAAFI, looking after the troops in Belfast.

Now that he has retired Alfie still keeps contact with his old Regiment, the Paratroop Regiment based in Aldershot, and in his room there is on display, for himself alone, an array of mementoes of his wartime service.

2000

Mrs Peggy Holding

- Millennium celebrations take place in the Millennium Dome.
- Jeffrey Archer is expelled from the Conservative Party for falsifying an alibi at a libel trial in 1987.
- A flotilla of boats crosses the English Channel from Dover to Dunkirk to commemorate the sixtieth Anniversary of the evacuation of Allied soldiers.
- Harold Shipman, Manchester GP, is sentenced to life imprisonment for murdering fifteen of his patients. Police believe he may have murdered over 150 people.
- The Rover car company is sold to the Phoenix Group by BMW for £1.
- In Zimbabwe, President Mugabe's proposed new Constitution is rejected in a referendum.
- Mr Mugabe is narrowly re-elected President of Zimbabwe after a disputed election.
- French footballer, Zinedine Zidane, who helped France to victory in the 1998 World Cup and Euro 2000, is voted the most popular person in France.
- Scotland's First Minister, Donald Dewar, dies.
- A Disputed Court decision in Florida during the US Presidential election leaves George Bush 930 votes ahead of Al Gore.

In 2000, Mrs Peggy Holding is now ninety-one. For the second time in two years, Peggy has suffered a broken leg. She has fought her way back to being able to walk again and still goes out to the shops.

THE TWELFTH CHILD

I was born on the 22nd June in 1909. My mother, my Maw as I ca'ed her, was just four months off fifty years of age when I was born. She was an old woman when I was born. She wore elastic-sided boots. And that was her with her shawl, her knittit napyen, as she called it. Aye, her napyen. She was a tidy old woman, with long hair. She kept it up in a bun at the back.

I was her twelfth. There was all the older ones, Andrew, Tommy, Mary, Isabella, that was Bella, and John and me, Peggy. I had two sisters died of the whooping cough when they were children, and there was others as died when they were babies. She was a wonderful woman, my mother. Her folks came from Skye, her mother, Mary McQueen. They're lying now in Sighthill Cemetery. But when they came to Scotland, they went to the Garngad, and that was where my mother was born. That's where she came from. We lived in Centre Street, up the wide pend, it was like Corporation hooses. I mind when she took me to the school at first the heidmaister said tae her, 'Tell the wee girl's mother to come and see me.' He thought my Maw was my Granny. And she said, 'I *am* her mother!' I went to school at Scotland Street School, it wasn't that long built. I was a bit of a tomboy. I used to go out with my gird, running wi' it, with the cleet.

My father, Andrew McCallum, was a boiler-maker. He went to Cuba to work, to make sugar-pans for them, for boiling the sugar. My Maw said he went off wi' a kist o' cla'es, and was away for five years. My Maw worked and reared my brothers. She used to dae the washing for the Janitor at Petershill School. She washed in the 'binie', the widden tub. My father was ill before he died. A year and five months she lifted and laid him. He was a big man, and she was just a wee buddy. When he was ill, she fed him on bananas, for she felt that would be good for him. And at the end she laid him out for his coffin.

THE FAMILY IN THE FIRST WORLD WAR

I had two brothers fought in the Army in the First War. Tommy and Andrew. They were Argylls, The Argyll and Sutherland Highlanders.

A kiltie Regiment, it was. Andrew was married with a family before he went off to the war. He lived in Aikenhead Road, and in the end he had nine of a family. But my brothers, they fought in France. I remember when I was just a wee girl, Andrew came back hame visiting. He'd been wounded. We flitted to 44 Cook Street. My Maw let oot hooses for the factor, she would look efter them, and let them oot. And we had the undertakers next to us, Hendersons, at the corner with Tradeston Street. Well, Andrew was back, he'd been wounded with shrapnel and was hame to recover. He was sitting by the windae, and he got me to see it. They came one night and took all Henderson's horses for the war. They were needed for the war so they came and took them. The horses were all sliding on the cossie stanes, and I could see the sparks flying from their hoofs. I couldnae believe it. The poor things, sliding on the stanes. But when he recovered, Andrew went back to the war and finished it. But he never said what it was like.

Then there was my youngest brother, John. John McCallum. He was my mother's only support, so they never took him into the Army. But then, in the end, they came for him. They needed him at the finish. And he died. He wanted only two days of twenty years of age. He was such a fine boy. My Maw had a wee self-sitting grate, he'd lean on it and play his mooth-organ. And he taught me to play it tae: we'd play together. John told my Maw, 'Don't worry. I'll no' be two months in the Army!' 'Oh John, you're no' going to disgrace your brothers by deserting,' she said. But he went off anyway, to train at Dunfermline. He died with lying on the pallet of straw. He caught double pneumonia, and he died. My Maw went to Dunfermline for his military funeral. The nurse told her 'He must've been very fond of you, for he was always singing *Mother Machree*. He sang it right through.'

When the war ended, they called it the Armistice, I mind there were a lot of people. And the people were out singing and dancing in the street.

CONFLICT IN IRELAND

I've seen all the wars. Even in Ireland. My sister, Bella, was married to Wullie Palfrey who came from Duke Street. He was killed in France in the First War, and Bella was left with a wee boy at just four months. Anyway my Maw reared the wee fellow. Then Bella met this fellow Alec Reardon, he was from Ireland, from Belfast, and they had two girls. One time I was over seeing them, and my sister went wi' me. We went on the boat from the Broomielaw. My maw had bought me a lovely new purple coat, but by the time we got to Belfast the water had shrunk it, and I couldn't fasten it. Over in Ireland, it was the troubles. And the bakery near where we were was bombed. It was in Burma Street, just off the Ormeau Road.

My two brothers were baith poulterers, baith o' them, so when I was growing up we never knew what it was to have to buy a chicken. Nae wonder the McCallums were big; the Holdings were all wee-made. When I was fourteen I left the school and went to work in Campbell Achnie's, the rubber works. I worked in the panning shop, where they boiled the rubber, to put it on the cloth for waterproofs. The lid of the big iron pan fell on me. They were going to take my airm off, it was so bad. But my Maw told the doctor, 'If she's going to die, she's going to die with her airm on.' And she took me hame and doctored me up. For six years she cured me, until I was twenty. And there was just one wee part that never healed up, never has, even to this day. And I used to go to the dancing, the National Halls in the Gorbals, and at the Hibernians.

FAMILY LIFE AND WAR AGAIN

I met my man in his auntie's: Henry Holding, Harry. He worked in Lairds, the box-makers, in Bridgeton. We were married in the Church in Buchan Street, and we lived in Carstairs Street. Lairds was just across the street. We were there for thirty-nine years. May was the first of my family. She was born in 1930. Then Charlie. When the war came, Harry was called up. He got his calling papers and he joined the Royal Air Force, the RAF. He worked with the Barrage Balloons, the big balloons that were to stop planes flying over. He used to get home on leave, and with us being just across the road from Lairds, the work would see him coming home. And then he was billeted in Springfield

Road School. And I mind one time there was one of his balloons came down right by the wash-hoose chimney, and the weans were all running daft, they were. And Harry was sent down from Springfield Road to get the balloon. [*After the Remembrance Service, when Peggy Holding was surrounded by people wanting to talk to her, a man came up and told her he had been one of the weans running after the balloon that day. He remembered how everyone stood and watched when men came to demolish the damaged wash-house chimney.*] He finished up abroad, in France and Belgium and Germany. In Belgium, his job was guiding boats, to stop them getting hit by planes. And he made real friends in Belgium, and at the end of the war they used to send me those special stockings, glass nylons. I mind the end of the war. I mind that bomb being dropped on Japan, and I knew that it was to draw people to their senses. But I don't think there'll ever be peace. Not in my time. Do you think it'll be in yours?

Harry was discharged from the RAF at last, and he came home with his kit-bag, and he went back to work. And in our wee single-end, in 74 Carstairs Street, I had all four of the children. Now there was Louis and Margaret, and I moved into my mother-in-law's house at number 88 when she moved out to Pollok. We came through hard times. In my poor days, I'd go to my Maw on a Saturday, and we'd have pie and beans, big beans, butter beans, the weans loved them. And I'd leave the weans wi' ma Maw, and I'd go to Sawyers for giblets. Do you know how much they cost? 4d [*2 pence*] a pound. I'd make barley and pea soup. I brought my children up on giblets, and I mind how Charlie used to sook the bones of the necks. But then Harry died in 1953. He was just eleven months older than me, and I was just forty-four then. I've been a widow for forty-seven years. And then we came out to Castlemilk, where I've been ever since.

THOUGHTS OF WAR AND THOUGHTS OF FAITH

I don't know what the Lord thinks of war. He has went through all the strife himself. He must have his thoughts. I was at church from a wee lassie. I went to Sunday School at Mr Symington's church in Kingston

Street. I went at eleven in the morning, and at two in the afternoon, and then again at five at night. When I was working, I got 8/8 pence [46 pence], and I got the 8d [3 pence] for my collection at the church. My Maw went to Mr Todd's wee mission along from the church. That was all the pensioners ever did. They went to the Missions, for they had nae guid cla'es for going to the church. But my Maw brought me up in the faith. I had a Bible she gave me.

And I brought my own family up in the Church too. And I've eleven grandweans and all the great-grandweans – I've seven great-grandweans, in America too.

But life's not been easy. Even when I was stabbed that time up in Mitchellhill, and needed eight stitches in my back. I got off the bus wi' my messages at the 37 terminus. And I got hit by what I thought was a stane. But it was a Stanley knife. I got eight stitches, but he got nothing. I held on to the messages and my pension book. And if you ask me what I thought aboot all that I just say, 'The Lord knows'. For I've always prayed to God. As I lie doon at night, I say 'Lord help me to get through to the morning.' I ask the Lord to bless them all, all my family, and all the poor ones in the world. And when I waken, it's just the same. 'Thank you, Lord for another day. And if you think I'm due another day, spare me to see it through.'

ARMISTICE SUNDAY

And so this is for Armistice Sunday is it? I mind that my friend Dolly Stevenson spoke on one of these Sundays. She and I grew up to be like sisters. I miss her still. But she's away now, to where the Lord's will is known, and she wouldnae change places wi' me. I'll be thinking of her on Armistice Sunday. And I think on my brother, John.

I don't know if I could be there on Sunday. I'll be on nettles, thinking, 'Oh dear me, people are listening to all this about me!'

Peggy McCallum, born on 22nd June 1909, married Harry Holding when she was nineteen, and she worked as a cleaner in Lairds, the box-makers, while bringing up their family. Harry served in the RAF during the war. When Harry died at the age of forty-five Peggy was left to bring up the family, May, Charlie, Louis and Margaret. Peggy could turn her hand to anything. She was a beautiful knitter, and she did all her own painting and decorating.

She was famous for always having sweeties: she would give them out at the shopping centre, at the church and to anyone she met. In her eighties she still enjoyed travelling to the United States to visit her son Louis and his family – in all, she made twelve trans-Atlantic trips to see them. In Scotland, she helped to bring up some of her grandchildren. When she was eighty-four, she was the victim of a shocking attack, but even though stabbed she fought back. In time, she overcame the effects of it all and kept her independent life. In February, 2001, her son, Charlie, died, a blow from which she never really recovered, and three months later Peggy herself died at the age of ninety-one.

2001

Mrs Elizabeth Hunter

- George Bush is sworn in as President of the United States of America.
- US and UK aircraft launch new strikes against military targets near Baghdad.
- British Prime Minister, Tony Blair, orders deployment of the Army to speed up the slaughter programme to stop the spread of foot and mouth disease.
- By the end of May, 3.2 million animals have been slaughtered to halt the spread of foot and mouth disease.
- Race riots in Bradford leave much destruction and many people injured, including 200 police.
- On the 11th September, terrorists linked to Saudi-born Islamic militant Osama bin Laden, mount devastating attacks with hijacked aircraft. Two are flown into the Twin Towers of the World Trade Center, one into the Pentagon building in Washington, and one crashed in open country in Pennsylvania.
- US and UK forces attack Taliban and Al Qaeda targets in Afghanistan.
- Human Genome project completed, with immense implications for biology and medical science.

In 2001 Mrs Elizabeth Hunter has been a widow for twenty-five years, and is the head of a large family. She worked for a private caterer as a waitress at evening functions until a few years ago, when she was eighty-one.

EARLY DAYS, HARD TIMES

I was born in 1914 – I was eighty-seven last month. I was born in Rosemount Street, just round from Roystonhill, born at home. But my oldest sister was sent out to our Auntie's at Riddrie. There was Nan, Mary, Pat, then me, and Hugh. But in between, my mother had still-births. My father died in Blochairn Steelworks. My brother, Hugh, was born in May 1916, and my father died in the August, in an accident at the works. He was up in the cran, and he was in one of those bucket things that hang, and sway. He was over a vat where they had the molten steel. My mother just said there was a terrible accident. She never said that he fell in. I don't remember him at all.

There was no widow's pension then. My mother had to go out to work – she worked in the munitions in Bishopton. My father had been exempt from the war through working in the steelworks. Before that, he had a wee barber's shop in Rosemount Street. He was a master-barber: that was what it said on Nan's birth lines and she was very proud of that.

It was in the poor times. There wasn't much money and then, after the war, it was harder to get the work. I knew times were hard. We didn't have warm clothes, no good footwear. We went barefoot many a time; from choice in the summer maybe, but in the winter we still didn't have shoes. Five of us my mother had to feed. She was a wonderful woman; big-made, red-haired with a temper to go with it: she'd let no-one stand in her way.

But then there was the Parish. If the Parish got hold of you, you had no chance. My mother had to do night work, and when she went out she left our Nan in charge. The neighbours said we wernae getting looked after. Someone put a report in. When I think back on it, it makes me wonder if I shouldn't just forget all about it. But it was very real for me.

FAR FROM HOME

I was ten. They took us away and we were taken into Stobhill Hospital. I knew that Hugh was there, but we were separated. They took me by train away up north, to Tomich, the other side of Beauly. Six weeks I was there, staying with an old lady. Then this day I came in and the old lady said, 'I've a surprise for you.' I went in and there was Hugh sitting on a big chair. I laughed and I cried, the way you do.

She was an elderly widow, and she had this wee house, and she had a big field, a park she called it, with potatoes. We ate potatoes all year round. We'd to help planting the potatoes, and we'd to help lifting them. We'd to turn the hay in the summer – she had another big field for her one cow, and she had several hens. Mrs Chisholm she was called. She had no gas or electricity, and we had to walk the cow to the park in the morning. I remember the time we both had the whooping cough. 'I'll cure you,' she said. A cup of milk, straight from the cow, hot and frothy. We had porridge every morning and night, thick soup at lunch-time. Occasionally she'd snare a rabbit for our dinner. That food's why I'm so healthy today, I think. We'd to walk to church each Sunday, about four miles.

There was a War Memorial in the middle of the village, just a big stone plinth, with a fountain and a well, with a cup on a chain. The horses went to the trough, but they always put their head in the basin of the fountain. We used to stand and watch that, and we used to stand at the Smiddy. We'd stand at the Smiddy for a heat, watching the blacksmith shoe the horses.

We had hard, rough clothes, sent from Glasgow. Boarded out children just got what was ordered: 'a sensible dress' nothing pretty or nice. Drab clothes; and boots. It marked you out. Those boots. And segs in your boots to make them wear. You'd to clean them too, and we didnae have your Cherry Blossom. No. Dubbin it was, to keep the snow out and the rain.

We were the only 'boarded out' children. We were ostracised. But we pushed ourselves on to learn as much as we could. The other children used to shout at us, 'Yer mother didn't want you!' 'Ye Boardie Outies!' But somehow we survived it. My beliefs helped me then. Later, when I was in England, I used to go to church every Sunday. Hughie used to say, 'God'll look after us, Liz. God'll look after us.' But strangely he lost his faith. He became an agnostic.

I used to hear from our sister, Nan, the odd letter. She told me that our mother had married again.

LEAVING SCHOOL, STARTING WORK

I left school at fourteen and worked for a school-teacher. I got three shillings a week and my keep, staying in the school-house. She had a child who I looked after when the school-teacher was in the school. I used to go to visit Mrs Chisholm on my days off.

Then I went to a shooting lodge, Jeevach [*Dhivaich*] Lodge near Drumnadrochit. They used to let it out for six to eight weeks for shooting and fishing. I was always left at the Lodge to make sure the Lodge was all right. There was the Falls of Dhivaich too, you could see them from the house. While I was there, Hugh came from Mrs Chisholm's and helped about the farm. Captain Smith that owned it taught Hugh to drive. So there we were, together again, Hugh and I.

I left there in February, 1932. It was a couple from Surrey that had come to the Lodge, more for the golf than for the fishing and shooting. When they were going back to Surrey their little girl said, 'Can't Elizabeth come to England with us?' Then in the October they wrote and asked Captain Smith if I wouldn't go. Then, in the February, I did go. I took the train from Inverness to Euston, the 'Ladies Only' compartment. About fourteen or fifteen hours. And there was a lot of sailors on the train, going to Portsmouth. I was as green as the grass. They had an accordion, and a mouth-organ. There was singing and dancing. It passed the journey. Then at the end one fellow said, 'I'm going to kiss you goodbye.' 'Indeed you are not,' said I. 'You're nothing but a wee bunch of stabby nettles,' said he.

I was fifteen months in Surrey. The man was a Colonel in the Army and he got called back to India and the wee girl Elspeth went with them. I went from Surrey to Sussex, working in big houses. It was an easy life. Three pounds a month was your wages, with your food and your bed. I worked at one big house near Epsom. That was where I was when Princess Marina got married, and they took us to London in

Daimlers and Lanchesters. And when King George V died, they took us up to see London in mourning. In between, on my holidays, I went to see Mrs Chisholm, and she was still taking in children, looking after the hens, milking her cow.

WIFE AND MOTHER IN WARTIME

I mentioned that Hughie became an agnostic. I don't know if the war did that for him or not. Hughie came home to Glasgow when the Smiths left Dhivaich. He came back to Glasgow and got a job at the big Exhibition. Then, in 1939, he joined the Air Force. He was good-looking in his uniform, with a mop of thick curly hair, slicked down with Brylcreem. He used to tell me about the war, how he was in Singapore, and they escaped by the skin of their teeth, and went to India. He was a Sergeant. My older brother, Pat, he was in the Army. But he never went overseas – he was over thirty by then.

I was in England for the beginning of the war. I was working at a house in the country. I heard on the wireless about it, the voice saying, 'Britain is at war'. And, at once, the sirens came on. Croydon was bombed. You saw the planes dropping their bombs, and you saw the smoke and the flames. They brought this big plane down in a field near Horsham, near where I was working. We all went up to see it the next day. It made you sad to see where the boys had died. I went to church each Sunday, and I used to say my prayers and wonder where the next bomb would fall. I wasn't in Scotland at the time of the Clydebank blitz, but we heard about it.

I was down in England, and they wanted me to go into work in the munitions in Surrey. My mother said, 'Come back up to Glasgow', and so I decided to go. And that was how I met Archie. He delivered the coal with a horse and cart. My sister, Nan, had been married for years to Joe Hunter. I went to visit them in Neptune Street in Govan. And this man was coming down the stair as black as night. And as he passed he said, 'You're my brother's sister-in-law.' And that was the start of it.

I had to go to the war effort. I went to work in the Co-operative Jam factory at Shieldhall. There were great vats of boiling jam, strawberry, blackcurrant, raspberry, all the fruits in season. I was working with the jars. I was always getting cut hands, cut fingers. But I was always independent.

When Archie and I started out, we were in rooms with Archie's sister: a single-end to the back, down the stair. In time, there was three weans and him and I, looking out to the dirty back. I hated it.

Eventually, Archie got called up for the Army, but he didn't do that long for the war tapered off. When Betty was born, I wasn't well; so Archie applied for an extension of leave. But it wasn't granted. So Archie just took it anyway. 'They'll come for me,' he said. But by then it didn't seem to matter so much. And he got demobbed with his suit and his hat. What a laugh it was.

In the war, we had the rations. I had four children by then, and you didn't get tea for the under-fives. But I got lots of sugar. So I'd trade sugar for tea. You could always barter. We never went without. As the children came along, I used to worry about the boys, that the war might go on and on, and that they might have to get caught up in it.

I remember hearing about the Atomic bomb in Japan. That was all so far away then. At the time we were living just off the Paisley Road West, near Cessnock. When the war ended, Archie went back to the coal. By now it was lorries, but since he wasn't a driver he was a carrier. It was heavy work, carrying coal to the top flat.

We got a house in Roystonhill, a big room-and-kitchen, and we had the children. There was Hugh, Archie, Betty, Pat, John, and Jeanette. We were only three minutes from the big church on the hill, and the boys were in the Lifeboys, and the girls were in the Sunday school. The Church was there and the nunnery was right next to it. The children took the bread and the potato peelings to feed the pigs in the Nunnery – where the elderly were kept. I think the Nunnery and the church are both away now. Only the steeple's still there from the church – and how they're keeping that up I don't know.

REMEMBRANCE DAY

When we were children up north, Remembrance Day was very strong in the schools. On the 11th, we did the two minutes' silence. We stood with our heads bowed and we all said the Lord's Prayer. I remember that teacher. We were told to think of all the soldiers who'd died in that war, and how they'd been badly led – they knew it was all wrong. I've often wondered if that young teacher had lost someone in it – she was so bitter about it. She made us learn the poem, 'The Charge of the Light Brigade.' 'Theirs not to reason why, theirs but to do and die …'

THE CASTLEMILK YEARS

In 1955, we moved out to Castlemilk. We were the first tenants of the house at 4 Machrie Road. We thought we were in heaven, from the room and kitchen in Roystonhill. But when Hughie, the oldest, was in his teens there was no work for him. So he joined the Army. I cried for a week, worrying about him. He was full of it, though. He took to it well, in the East Anglian Regiment. He went to Germany, and he drove big trucks. But then he had a terrible accident on the autobahn. They didn't think he was going to live. He was married in Germany, his wife was in the Army too. He did recover, but he had screws in his ankle, and he couldn't drive the big lorries any more. But rather than have just a desk job, he took his pension. And I was relieved when he came out.

And here we are again with war going on, and you think of the young ones, and of the innocent ones suffering.

I've spoken quite a lot. And I'll be listening to what you say. And if I'm not happy with it, you know you'll have to answer to *me*!

***

Elizabeth Hunter raised a large family, and there were hard times when the children were young. Mr Hunter worked collecting scrap, in his early days it was with a horse and cart. Elizabeth, Betty, steadily carried the joys

and sorrows in the life of a big family. Though small of stature, she always had a regal air about her: she had a great sense of humour, but her dignified way of relating to people was reminiscent of the Queen Mother. Before the Sunday on which these words were read to the congregation, she had never spoken of her childhood and wartime memories. Her children knew that her early years had not been easy, but she had told them nothing. Her decision to allow people to hear about her childhood enabled her own children to understand her better and to admire her even more than before.

For over thirty-five years, she worked many evenings and weekends as a waitress with a firm of private caterers. She loved meeting new people, and enjoyed celebrations of all kinds. She was a person in whom others could confide, and she had a great understanding for waifs and strays and people in trouble. In May, 2002, as was fitting for such a family-centred person, she died peacefully at home surrounded by members of her family.

2002

Mr Joseph Barclay

- The Euro becomes the official currency across eleven countries in Europe – the largest single currency area in Europe since the days of the Roman Empire.
- Princess Margaret dies in February.
- Queen Elizabeth, the Queen Mother, dies in March aged 101 and her televised funeral is watched by millions worldwide.
- Foreign Secretary, Jack Straw, states that Baghdad's 12,000-page declaration of its weapons programme is 'a blatant lie'.
- Moors murderer, Myra Hindley, dies aged sixty following a respiratory infection.
- Northern Ireland Assembly suspended after claims that an IRA spy-ring has been uncovered at the Northern Ireland Office.
- Trial of Royal butler, Paul Burrell, collapses after it emerges that he had told The Queen in 1997 that he had taken items belonging to Princess Diana for safe keeping.

In 2002, Mr Joseph Barclay is still carrying many responsibilities. His wife Jessie suffers from Alzheimer's and Joe looks after her. He has his car and they visit the family regularly. Joe always dresses immaculately, with collar and tie, and shoes shining.

CHILDHOOD IN THE GORBALS.

December the 4th, 1923, I was born. We stayed in a room and kitchen at 24 South Shamrock Street in the Gorbals. My father had fought in the First World War. He was in the Argyll and Sutherland Highlanders, and he had been wounded in the left arm at the Battle of Mons. The scar on his arm was prominent, I remember, and you would see it every time he was washing himself. In these days you would wash yourself down in the black sink in the corner or in the zinc bath in front of the fire. You could see that the muscle on his arm was practically blown out altogether. But none of the family ever commented on it. And my father never ever mentioned anything about the war. He had several medals, and when he died my older brother, John, got them. I don't know where they'll be now. My father worked as a 'rid leeder' in the shipyards, painting the inside of the hulls with the red-lead paint against the rust. There was four boys and three girls in that room and kitchen: Margaret, John, me, Jim, Nan, Terry and George. Then we moved into Errol Street when my mother's mother died, and we stayed with my grandfather. My mother lost a brother in the war. He was an Argyll as well, and there was a picture of him in the room, a massive picture, two foot by eighteen inches. I always admired my Dad: he came right home on a Friday and gave my mother the wages before he went out. We never wanted for anything. He lived to be about eighty, and he was always concerned about the family. But my grandfather was fierce and my Dad had no life with him, so my Dad went and lived in a model lodging house. My mother was a hawker, going round the big houses collecting the old clothes and she sold them at the Briggait at the Saltmarket, under the Arches. In those days, Paddy's Market was in the lane at Commercial Road, and from the age of about ten I used to sweep the lane on Tuesdays and Saturdays, and I got a penny for it, and I used to help the hawkers to tie up their bags of rags.

I wasn't at all religious-minded when I was young. I never went to chapel of my own free will. Jim and John and myself and Nan, when we were that wee bit older, we'd be sent off to chapel on the Sunday.

Us boys would send Nan into the chapel to find out what the priest was wearing and what colour cloth was on the Altar, but the three of us boys would go down to the Clyde and go on one of Geddes's boats. And in the summer holidays, when you were supposed to get a ticket each Sunday and give the six tickets to your teacher when school began, we'd go in to the chapel and get our ticket at the door; then one of us would 'take ill' and the rest of us, we'd all bring that one back out.

EARLY WORKING DAYS

I left school at fourteen and went to work at 248 Cumberland Street as a message boy at Frank Stewart's the butchers. They supplied the Army and Navy Stores with butcher meat. My route was King's Park, where Mickle and McTaggart were just finishing building the bungalows. You'd never believe what they cost: they were selling at £420. There was a delivery bike for a message boy, but I never grew enough to reach the pedals, so I had to go out on the bus. There'd be ten or twelve parcels of meat, well over a stone in weight, and the name was written on each, on the brown paper wrapping it. Then I became the sausage boy: making links, Lorns, and round sliced, and the mince. I could do it all by the finish.

Next, I went to work in Harland and Wolffs as an apprentice plumber – I just walked in with my pal, Robert McCallum, and we asked if they wanted any apprentices. But that first year they never taught me anything, just sent me errands to get washers and things. So the day I was seventeen I walked out, went and got myself a Provisional licence, and went to drive a van for A. F. Reid, the bakers, in Victoria Road. Then there was better money working with Balfour Beattie, and I went up to the Orkney Islands working in the Quarry, where they were blasting rock for making the new runway for the aerodrome. It was 1942, and I knew I was going to be called up for the Army. And I had terrible sweaty feet and whenever I had to walk any distance they got red raw. So to stay out of the Army, I volunteered for the Navy.

INTO THE ROYAL NAVY

My first leave home from the Orkneys, I got two letters the same day. My Army medical appointment, and my call-up papers for the Navy. Off to the Navy I went. John and Jim came with me on the tram from Errol Street to Central Station and waved me away. I was off down to Great Malvern for six weeks' on-shore training. Drill, square-bashing, rifle drill, the knots, the various small arms. At this time you didn't know whether, when you went to a ship, you'd be up above, as a seaman, a gunner, a signal-man, or down below in the engine room or stuck in the galley as a chef.

I was assigned to Devonport, to the destroyer the *Campbeltown*, and I was a stoker in the engine room. Our job was to escort the convoys of merchant ships across the Atlantic and across the Baltic Sea. I remember the very first time. We left London, and sailed round the south coast and up the West, and we came and picked up our convoy up by Oban at the anchorage there, and we headed for Murmansk in Russia. I'd never heard of Murmansk or Archangel, which was the two places we made for. I did six convoys to Murmansk. I lost count of the number of times we crossed the Atlantic. When we went across the Atlantic, there was one dreaded part we went through. Three hundred square miles. They called it 'The Black Hole', 'U-boat Alley'. At that time it was out beyond the range of aircraft cover, and the U-boats lay in wait. We lost a terrible lot of ships there.

But this time we were on the Russian convoy. Just before we reached Bear Island the U-boat pack was there. We dropped depth charges, but all of a sudden there was this huge explosion. The torpedo had hit us. I'd never heard anything like it. At once, the ship took on huge quantities of water, and the order came to abandon ship. I headed as fast as I could up on to the deck, and I was assigned to a Carly-float. It was a kind of float with ropes attached, which twenty men could hold on to in the water. And you had your life-jacket on, your Mae West we used to call it, which could keep you afloat for seventy-two hours. Two men dropped the float over the side and held it in place with ropes. Then we jumped into the water, it was quite a drop, and you moved the Carly-float away from the side of the ship. It was night time, but it was amazing how you could see. And now, after we'd got off, the flames came. Then came the explosion, and she just disappeared. Quite a few hands were lost. I was a swimmer, but you had your life-jacket on, too, your Mae West. Others had rubber life belts which you had to inflate. We were in the water for four hours, when a trawler came to pick us up. 'A coffin ship', we called them. For they had to be stationary so as to pick you up, and they were a sitting duck if the U-boats were still around. But the U-boats weren't bothering about survivors that day. They were away after the merchant-men. After that, we got seven days Survivors' Leave, and then we were assigned to another ship and back to sea.

PREPARING FOR D-DAY

I think one sinking is enough to give them. I had four sinkings altogether. Two of them were when I was on Motor Torpedo Boats, MTBs. We were based at Lowestoft, the most easterly edge of England. I was a driver, then. I went on a course to drive them. They called you a Stoker ICE. A stoker on Internal Combustion Engines. The boat had three Rolls Royce Merlin engines, 500 horse-power. You cruise on two of them, then when you went into attack you went in with all three. You could do forty-two knots. Our MTBs were made of triple ply-wood. It made us very fast, and very buoyant, being the wood. But when you were up against the German E-Boats, which were made of steel, you could be in trouble.

Intelligence would tell us what ships were our target, and off we'd go – day or night. They would tell us where the target was. It might be at sea or in harbour. And if it was in harbour we'd cruise in on two engines, strike, and run out again on the three engines at full speed. You would say to yourself, 'Am I going to come out of this?' Then you learned to take every day as it came. Then you took every day as a bonus. Sometimes they told us to go and attack in Cherbourg harbour. We hated Cherbourg. It has three harbours, and your target was always in the inner one. Twice I was on MTBs that were sunk, and twice I was rescued.

My last ship was called the *Ficho* – a French word for rabbit. It was the oddest looking ship you'd ever seen. With thirty-one of a crew, it was a Dan-layer, marking the channels that other ships were to take. We set sail on June the 2nd 1944 at two a.m., destination unknown, and under sealed orders. When the Old Man opened the orders it said we were to sail to the French Coast, to Normandy, to Arromanches, to mark out the channels for the invasion fleet. We set the markers, buoys held in place by concrete linked by cables, and the barges and what were known as the Mulberry Harbours would come in that way. When we heard what we were to do we said, 'We'll never make it.' As we set out, I really thought we were gone. We went across the Channel, and we were seen as we did it all in broad daylight. There was a lot of men lost. There were commandos on shore as well, but we called ourselves Churchill's Dirty Job Men. I was still a driver, and the *Ficho* was right inshore marking the channels when she was hit by the shore batteries. After the explosion there was a massive hole in the ship. There wasn't a great deal left of the deck. Into the water you went.

I was never wounded. I had begun to think that someone up there liked me. I lost very, very many people I knew. There was nothing you could do for them. Into the water. I survived the cold. You didn't give a thought to dying. You're looking for a ship, and you wouldn't care if it was an enemy ship or your own. This time it was another small boat, no name, only numbers. He was coming back across the Channel to Falmouth. From Falmouth we went to Devonport where we were given fourteen days leave. And when I came back they put me on a mine-layer going to the Far East. But that's not a good story. The action we were in was terrible. I'm not going to tell you about it.

THINKING ABOUT WAR

Oh yes. There's an awful lot had an awful lot more than me, I can assure you of that. At least I got home in one bit, never wounded, never a scratch.

I remember we went to Hiroshima, just about ten days after they dropped the bomb on it. You never seen devastation like it, as far as the eye could see. Only the strongest stuff was still standing, beams and stuff, but no buildings. Nothing left. Nothing to see. Scorch-marks where there had been bodies. I thought at the time, 'It's brilliant to get the war finished. But I hope one never comes near me!'

I don't know why they dropped that second bomb on Nagasaki. A threat would have been sufficient after that. They were on the brink of surrender. We met the Japanese, for me and Midge Lindsay from Edinburgh we would go to the YMCA or to a local church. You were always sure of a good meal, and they took good care of you. You see, I said that I never went to chapel of my own free will. But I'd changed. Going into my first action I found myself saying a prayer. And the padre gave me a set of rosaries which I carried all through the war. I kept them in the rule pocket of my overalls, so they were always with me. Then I got a Bible off a man in a Church in Colombo in Ceylon, Sri Lanka as it is now. I carried it from then on, and then I gave it to my son, Billy, when he went to sea.

When the war was finished, we stayed out in the Far East. We were mine-sweeping round Hong Kong, Malaya, the Malacca Straits; any known mine-fields we were clearing them. We were on a Brooklyn's Yard minesweeper, BYMS 2017. We'd collected it from the yard in New York. I was still a Stoker ICE, until I was demobbed in September 1946, more than a year after the war ended.

I ended the war more religious than I started it. Yes, most definitely. Otherwise I wouldn't be in your church every Sunday. And I look forward to going every Sunday. I seldom watch war films. Some of them annoy me – especially how easy they make things seem.

REMEMBRANCE SUNDAY

When I was at school, we had the silence on the 11th of November. We sat at our desks for two minutes. We didn't really realise what we were sitting there for. But when Remembrance Day comes now, it brings back an awful lot that you don't want to remember. But it comes back anyway. Jessie's sister lost her husband in the war. And I have personal friends I remember on Remembrance Sunday. Quite a few. You always attach to someone when you join another ship, and they usually turn out to be good friends.

This is the first time I've told anyone about what happened in the war. Even Jessie hasn't heard it. But I think that'll do. I think there's ample there.

———— ««»» ————

After the war, Joe Barclay worked with the Glasgow Corporation. He was a foreman with the Highways Department, in charge of the Mobile Squad. This group of men were despatched to all emergency problems – holes appearing in the road, unexpected subsidences, flood damage. They were something of a law unto themselves, and had a reputation for being extremely resourceful. Joe enjoys reminiscing about the enterprises and escapades in which he became involved. The abilities which were developed during the years of war were put to constant use in his working life. But he has enjoyed his retirement years, also.

He is a family man, proud of his family and grand-children. In recent years, his wife, Jessie, has suffered from Alzheimer's disease and Joe has been her principal carer. In the autumn of 2003, their house went on fire. Somehow Joe managed to rescue Jessie from the smoke and they both escaped through a window. Even yet he is a man to rely on in a crisis.

2003

Mrs Agnes Wilson

- An outbreak of Severe Acute Respiratory Syndrome (SARS) in China reaches epidemic proportions and claims lives as far away as Canada.
- Biggest-ever protest takes place in London, with 750,000 marching in opposition to war with Iraq.
- Dr Rowan Williams is installed as the 104th Archbishop of Canterbury.
- US and British troops invade Iraq to eliminate weapons of mass destruction and to achieve a change of regime.
- J. K. Rowling's latest book, *Harry Potter and the Order of the Phoenix* becomes the fastest-selling book of all time, at 500 per minute in the first hour of sale.
- The Roslin Institute announces that Dolly the sheep, ageing prematurely, has been put down.
- Space Shuttle *Columbia* disintegrates on re-entry to earth's atmosphere, killing all seven astronauts on board. NASA is accused of ignoring warnings of imminent disaster.
- Russian billionaire Roman Abramovich buys Chelsea Football Club for £59.3 million.
- Though President Bush announced on 2nd May that 'major combat operations' in Iraq were at an end, by the year's end civil unrest in Iraq was a growing problem.

In 2003, Mrs Agnes Wilson still lives in the Castlemilk house to which she and her husband and her father and her brothers moved in 1955. She remains the centre of the life of her family and grandchildren.

THE OUTBREAK OF WAR

I'll never forget the morning war broke out. I was just getting ready to go to Church. My mother had gone to the dairy to get something. I could hear her from three stairs up. I knew she'd gone out to the dairy, and the next thing I heard was sobs and greets from my mother, 'That's my sons, that's my sons!' She had five sons. My Da had been in the First World War, and she had lost her twin brother Andrew – he'd been drowned in it – was it in Boston? My Da had been wounded in the left leg, just as my brother John was to be wounded in the next war. My Da always had a sort of limp. It was the calf of his leg. He was always a carter, and in the Army he was with the Scottish Horse. He loved horses, my Dad. There wasn't a lazy bone in his body: he was a hard-working man. 'Where there's a will there's a way,' he'd say. Then he worked in the tyre company over at Inshinnan, up at all hours of the morning. I'm awful proud of my family I must say.

He'd sometimes speak of the war as we grew up. My mother would always tell him to stop. But if he got a drink on a Saturday he'd sing. And he'd take me between his legs and he'd tell us about the war. The hard biscuits they got, and how they'd say to each other 'We'd be as well eating them for we don't know if we'll be here tomorrow.' Then he'd sing wee songs, like

> *If it wisnae for Paddy and Sandy*
> *Where would proud England be?'*

And it's the same to this day. England still relies on Scotland and Ireland.

VOLUNTEERS FOR SERVICE

You know, I can always remember my mother saying once before the war that she was glad when she heard it was a boy she'd had, because they have an easier time of it. When they come in at the end of the week they just wash their face, put on a clean shirt and tie, and out they go.

Whereas women had everything to do all the time. But then the war came. All my brothers were volunteers, every one of them. I'm so sorry for women that's got all sons. It's no' easy if you've a family of sons, where war is concerned. I used to cry myself to sleep each night. I'd shed tears for my mother's sorrow. My nights were spent writing letters to them: my mother would get me to write to them all. Oh, war's a terrible, terrible thing. For I knew my mother's feelings. I felt the same. I loved my brothers dearly, so I did. I was in the middle, born after Andrew, with the three brothers younger than me.

My mother had six sons. Her first-born was a wee William, Billy. Wee Billy took meningitis at thirteen months. My Da was away in the war, fighting at Salonika, not there when the wee one died. Then there was John, and Andrew, and James. Then Tommy. And Billy – he got the name of wee one that had died. He was the youngest of the boys, and when the war started he was an evacuee. John had a wee car in 1939, and he took Billy one Sunday when he was evacuated to Inverurie. But the following week, they'd to go back and fetch him – Billy wanted in beside us all again. He'd been John's van-boy in Beatties', the bakers. But he volunteered before the war was over, and got shell-shocked, blew up in the Black Forest. Young ones nowadays don't realise how lucky they are. My brothers never had a youth. They went away boys and came back men.

My mother loved her sons, adored them. They were all that good. Their hearts were as tender as a woman's. At first of course, when you're wee, they pull yer hair. But when we got older there wasn't one of them wouldn't give you everything – we were all very close to each other – a devoted family. We felt each other's pain. We stayed at 33 Glenlyon Street, three stairs up. It was a room and kitchen with the eight of us. We were lucky that had a room-and-kitchen: We were born in a single-end in Bluevale Street, a low-down house to the front.

They weren't easy times. My Daddy was quick tempered, but got over it as quick; and my mother, I can mind of it, she was stubborn and wouldn't answer. And she'd keep it up. I think I spent my childhood in tears. At the Orange Walk I was terrified. Everything came ower the windaes. The only one up our close that wisnae the same as us was Mrs Flanagan. And Mrs Flanagan knew that my mother had that many of us, and she stood at the City Bakers for a cream cake for my mother. And my father always had a quarter gill for Mrs Flanagan. My Da's old aunt stayed up the one stair, and she'd save up all the cigarettes for the boys coming home on leave. Yet when we were young she was never away from shouting at us for making a noise.

We were really close as a family: one for all and all for one. And my Dad, he had great respect for his sons. Even if he was angry at something he'd never rebuke them in front of a third party.

THE BOYS AT WAR

John

John volunteered for the Army. He was captured at Tobruk. We never knew what had happened to him. The first word we got was that he was missing. And we never knew what to think. Then we got a post card from him, telling us no to worry – he was fine – he was a prisoner of war. They took him away to Poland. And John walked a thousand miles from Poland to Germany. They marched them a thousand miles in sleet and snow. I remember the day he was repatriated. He came home, and he went down on his knees and put his arms round my mother's waist. And he told her that but for her he wouldnae ha' been here. It was all the rough feeding she'd given us, the porridge and the tripe, and the mince and tatties, that had made him so strong. On that long march they'd been dropping like flies at the roadside beside him in the snow.

He's in California now, and I know how much he'd like to come back and visit Glasgow again, but he's not able for the journey.

Andrew

Andrew wanted into the Navy. He volunteered for the submarines. And he had a terrible time. He lost such a lot of mates in the submarines. But he never spoke about it. He was here earlier this year, and just last month he got the Freedom of Stoke for all that the submarines did. And I asked him what he'd done. He said he was at the torpedoes. He served on the *Superb*, and the *Tuna*, and he was on the *Trenchant*. He was on an operation in Norway, taking midget submarines. They made five hits on their eight targets and sank a lot of shipping. They sank other U-boats. They were over in the Pacific, too, and sank a heavy Japanese cruiser, and a ship loaded with rubber. Two of his commanders got VCs, Commander Campbell and Commander Price. And Andrew himself got the DSM, the Distinguished Service Medal, for his own part in things. But he wouldn't tell me anything about it.

James

James volunteered for the Navy, too. He served on destroyers. He was a stoker, shovelling the coal. He'd been transferred, once, from a destroyer that was sunk just days after he left it. My cousin, David Bruce, who'd visited us in Glasgow the week before, he went down with it. War's a terrible thing when there's men in the family. James was two years in Malta, then he was away in the Pacific. He was there when the war ended. My mother had been very ill. James came home the day before she died. She died on Christmas Day at five minutes to three, just as the King was going to speak on the radio. Then the day after my mother's funeral, James's girlfriend packed him in – she'd been going with someone else while he'd been away. It took James a long time to settle down when he came back. He couldn't sit, and he'd keep late hours. He just couldn't settle.

Tommy

There was only eleven months between James and Tommy. I felt so sorry for Tommy. He was in a reserved occupation in Sir William Arroll's, an engineer, electrical engineer, and they widnae let him go. They were making guns and armaments for the war. And he felt terrible with his four brothers all in the forces. He was at home all of the war. But he was hardly at home. He was working night and day, long, long shifts all the time. He'd have to walk to work. My Dad was a fire-fighter, when the sirens went he had to go out too.

Billy

By the end of the war, Billy was old enough to be a soldier, and he volunteered and joined the Seaforths. But he wasn't long in it when they were thrown right into things, with no right training or anything. They were in the Black Forest, and they were blown up. Billy had a scarred leg. And he was shell-shocked and he was put into the hospital. By the time he came home he was more or less back to himself. But, you know, my brothers never ever told you very much about the bad things that happened to them.

THE GIRL IN THE FAMILY

I'd worked myself in Patersons' Cleansil works in Orr Street, off the Gallowgate. I was making everyday cleaning products, like Parazone and washing liquid. It was a terrible time. You were aye writing letters, but if you heard from one you never heard from the others. I used to go to the Church, St Thomas's the UF Church in the Gallowgate.

One of the boys I worked with there, John Waters, was in the Army, and I wrote to him and sent him parcels. He told me he'd a mate who was feeling lonely, and would I write to him? So Joe Wilson wrote to me and I wrote to him. On their next leave, John Waters and Joe Wilson, and a Dougie something, all came home together. The other two had girlfriends, and we all hit it off. I think on our third meeting we got married. A whirlwind it was. We met in October, then three days at the New Year, then we married on the 9th of April, when Joe got embarkation leave before going to India. He proposed by letter. The first letter never arrived, but I think I know what happened to that one. My mother wasnae wanting to part with me. But I got the second one. My mother said, 'No way!' My Dad turned round and said, 'Write and tell him, "Father says, 'Yes'; Mother says, 'No'"!' My Da always liked Joe. I was Joe's first girlfriend, too.

After we married – that was 1941 – he didn't have to go to India right away. We stayed with his sister in Airdrie. Myra was born after that.

But, by then, he was away in India, and he never saw Myra till she was two-and-a-half. And if ever I heard of a couple who married and then stayed together I thought it was wonderful, not having the man leaving again after just a couple of days.

PEACETIME LIFE BEGINS AGAIN

There's an awful lot of memories that were bad. You put them away to the back of your mind. It's as if you were putting it in a drawer or a cupboard and shutting the door on it. But I can always mind the joyous feeling when peace was declared. There had been rumours about the peace beforehand. But we were so happy. It was wonderful when we heard the news. We had parties, dancing in the streets. They cried them 'clabbers'. We had a big spare field facing us, up near where Bernie McQuade stayed. We had the clabbers there. It was good. We had dancing, bonfires, the lot. Margaret McDonald stayed just along the street – I remember the man she married. And Margaret Brown stayed in Slatefield Street off the Gallowgate – I remember Joe and me walking Myra down that way.

When the war was finished, James was in the Pacific, and he didn't get home for months. But after the war, they all did different things. I looked after my father and my brothers, Joe and I and Myra stayed with them. We were offered a house out in Cranhill, but it was too near the canal for me, and too near Barlinnie Prison. The next offer was Castlemilk, and that was us: Joe, my Dad, and Andrew, Tommy and James. Five men in the house they were.

John's house in Glasgow was bombed in the war and there wasn't much to come back to. When he was a prisoner of war in Poland, the only books he had were on gardening. He'd been a van-man before the war but now he and a mate started up in a little nursery and market garden in Ardrossan. He worked from early morning to late at night. But it was hard to make a living at it. He studied to be a draughtsman, and he went out to California and prospered.

Andrew worked in the Post Office until retirement, he delivered in Duke Street.

James got into Arrolls Steelworks in Dunn Street. Tommy worked in Arrolls's for a long number of years and then moved to Scotts in Anderston.

Billy went to work in the Chemical work, he got a job there for my uncle used to be the manager.

Joe worked in Godfrey Davis, he travelled all the way over to Airdrie every day.

THE FAMILY AND WAR

I never had sisters, you see. So having a daughter was wonderful, that was Myra. Then there was Alison, a sister for Myra, I was that glad for her she had a sister. Then Nan – she was beautiful when she was born. And then Irene, the youngest. It's hard being the youngest. She's so good to me. They're all so good to me.

Now we've got this latest war. Oh my. All these poor women. Their sons are there. Their hearts'll be broken. I always remember Cathy Barclay's man singing *A Scottish Soldier*. Now his ain grandson's there –

> *Though fair and green these foreign hills may be,*
> *They are not the hills of home.*

All my life there's been war. I don't know if there'll ever be a time without war. Man seems so greedy for power. It's about greed and power. And young men do what they think is right, fighting for freedom, fighting for King and country. And when I think on it, I wanted to go, too. One of my pals was in the WAAFs [*Women's Auxiliary Air Force*], another in the ATS [*Auxiliary Territorial Service*]. I'd have liked to go to the WAAFs. But when I spoke of it my Ma dissolved in tears and I knew I couldnae.

It's not Jesus who's wanted this war, not his fault. I think Jesus is up there breaking his heart over what men do to each other.

All through those times you always prayed to God to keep your brothers safe, and to give your mother strength to bear it all.

For where else would we get the strength to bear all these things?

When the war was over, and her husband, Joe, returned from service in the forces, Agnes looked after her household of five men and her own growing family. She did everything for her husband and her brothers and her father, even cleaning their working boots for them every day. After her brothers married, and her father died, she continued doing everything for her four daughters. She was a member of the Young Mothers' Club in the church, and each week she used to go to the pictures with her sister-in-law. In addition she worked as a domestic cleaner, and for twenty years she worked part-time in a local Home for the elderly, as an auxiliary, doing the full range of care work.

Having grown up as the only girl with her six brothers, Agnes was delighted to be the mother of four daughters. Now the next generation has boys again: she has nine grandsons and one grand-daughter, and she has two great-grandsons. Agnes continues to be at the centre of her family's life.

POSTSCRIPT

So ends a series of encounters with men and women who have witnessed and taken part in historic events, but whose voices are seldom heard. Selected virtually at random from within a working-class Glasgow community, they exemplify, like their counterparts across the world, a life recognisably heroic.